Truth Seeker:
BIBLE TOPICS

Your beauty should not come from outward adornment, such as braided hair and fine clothes. Instead, it should be that of your inner self, the unfading beauty of a gentle and quiet spirit, which is of great worth in God's sight. (1Pe 3:3-4)

Truth Seeker:

BIBLE TOPICS

Third Edition

Warren M. Mueller

iUniverse, Inc.
Bloomington

Truth Seeker: Bible Topics
Third Edition

Copyright © 2013 Warren M. Mueller

iUniverse books may be ordered through booksellers or by contacting:

iUniverse
1663 Liberty Drive
Bloomington, IN 47403
www.iuniverse.com
1-800-Authors (1-800-288-4677)

ISBN: 978-1-4759-8172-8 (sc)
ISBN: 978-1-4759-8174-2 (hc)
ISBN: 978-1-4759-8173-5 (e)

Library of Congress Control Number: 2013904760

Printed in the United States of America

iUniverse rev. date: 3/26/2013

Dedication

To my Lord Jesus, who has provided the inspiration
and revelation for this book;

To my wife, Diane, who is God's greatest gift to me
besides himself;

To my wonderful children, Mindy and Jacob;
who are blessings from God.

To Dylan, Kaden, and Kylie, precious grandchildren
and source of many wonders and renewed youth.

Contents

Foreword

By Kevin Fontaine, PhD

These days we live in a "Bizarro World." Comic book fans will recall the "Bizarro World" in the Superman Comics. This world was upside-down and backwards in that alarm clocks dictate when to go to sleep, ugliness is beautiful, evil is good and good is evil. Even the casual observer of our culture would be hard pressed to argue that our age is marked by clear and consistent moral integrity and understanding of the difference between right and wrong. Quite simply we have lost our way and we are sinking fast! Our move toward moral relativism with its view that there are no objective moral standards to determine what is right or wrong is literally killing our society. It's a cancer that is eating us alive because moral relativism makes lying, cheating, infidelity, and the killing of unborn children legitimate forms of personal expression. It's our version of the "Bizarro World." If it feels right do it and to hell with the consequences.

That's why Warren Mueller's "Truth Seeker: Bible Topics" is so timely and important. He effectively lays out what the Bible tells us in relation to over 30 of the most important issues and subjects that confront our culture. With topics ranging from abortion to the viewing of pornography, Mr. Mueller provides cogent, yet comprehensive explanations of the truths that saturate each and every page of the Bible. In other words, Mr. Mueller has taken on the Herculean task of combing through the Bible to see what it says to us about the issues that confront each of us every day. Mr. Mueller performs this near impossible task with grace and aplomb.

I know that I will keep a copy of "Truth Seeker: Bible Topics" at hand and will dive into it frequently, especially when confronted with a situation that requires the wisdom and guidance that can only come from God's Word.

Kevin Fontaine is Assistant Professor of Medicine in the Division of Rheumatology at the Johns Hopkins University School of Medicine. A Health Psychologist whose research focuses on the physical and emotional consequences of living with chronic diseases, he is the author of over 60 scientific articles and book chapters on topics such as health psychology, obesity, epidemiology, and arthritis. Dr. Fontaine also is the author of two Christian books, "Living the Fruit of the Spirit: Lessons from Barney Rubble" and "The Jesus Cure: The 4 Keys to Living a Life of Integrity, Significance, and Peace."

Acknowledgements

I would like to thank my father, Frank Mueller, for his example and encouragement to search out the truth in all things through self-study and independent thinking. I am very grateful for the mentoring I have received from many Christians over the years: to Joseph Rains who showed me the Way through the Bible; to my first pastor, Stuart Briscoe, for the excellent foundation in Biblical instruction I received through his sermons and writings; to Brian and Bobbie Burns and their small group members with whom I experienced the unconditional wonder of Christian fellowship and love and to Walter Holst and Ernest Cochran who have strengthened my faith through their example. Finally, I would like to thank my pastor, Tony Casoria, for taking the time from his busy schedule to review this book.

Introduction

The purpose of this book is to summarize what the Bible says about frequently asked subjects. It is my belief that the Bible is a reliable source of wisdom and contains truth that God has given to mankind to guide us through life.[1] I have found that these truths can be discovered by a systematic study of the Bible. It is not necessary to have a theology degree to interpret the Bible. All that is needed is a personal faith in Jesus as the Christ, which produces a spiritual birth and results in the indwelling presence of the Holy Spirit who counsels and guides believers.[2]

Christian books and doctrines can be valuable resources to assist in spiritual understanding, but there is no substitute for daily, individual study of the Bible. Indeed, these resources can become stumbling blocks to a vibrant, personal relationship with God, as they represent the experiences or beliefs of others. Many Christians have opted to fill their minds with these experiences and thoughts of others, which results in religious beliefs that are learned rather than personal truths

---

1   Your Word is a lamp to my feet and a light for my path. (Ps 119:105)

2   But when he, the Spirit of Truth, comes, he will guide you into all truth. He will not speak on his own: he will speak only what he hears, and he will tell you what is yet to come. (Jn 16:13)

experienced from the revelation of an encounter with God in his Word. This tends to result in denominational Christians who, like the Israelites, prefer to have Moses or their priests en-counter God and interpret his will rather than experience for themselves. Christianity is primarily not about religious doctrines, but rather a continuing personal experience of God, resulting in the transformation of the mind which, in turn, changes thoughts and behavior.

This book attempts to explain some of the truths of the Bible that are relevant to our human nature, thoughts, and purpose. I believe that much of the controversy surrounding what the Bible says stems from a lack of systematic study, taking verses out of context, or attempting to extrapolate truth beyond what is clearly stated. In order to avoid these pitfalls and optimize a fair interpretation, the following principles are used in this book:

1. Truth is progressively revealed, and, therefore, some portions of the Old Testament have been superseded by the New Testament. One example is that the Old Testament animal sacrifices for sins have been replaced by the perfect sacrifice of Jesus Christ, once, for all the sins of mankind. Where there has been no further revelation on a particular subject, I believe that the Old Testament truths are God's final words and are relevant to us today. An example of this is found in Leviticus 19:28 where tattooing is forbidden. Nothing more on this subject is mentioned in later books of the Bible, and, therefore, I believe that this prohibition is God's revealed will on this subject.

2. Since God does not contradict Himself, the correct meaning of passages of the Bible that seem to conflict is achieved by comparing the unclear verses with others that address the same subject. For example, James 2:14-17 seems to say that man's good works play a role in salvation. This appears to be in conflict with other verses in the Bible, such as Ephesians 2:8-9; Titus 3:5, and Romans 6:23,

which say that salvation is by faith alone. How are these verses reconciled? It is accomplished by referring to other Bible verses that say that those who believe and receive Jesus Christ as their personal savior experience a spiritual birth, become children of God, and are transformed by the Holy Spirit, who indwells them to do good works.[3] In order to understand what the Bible says on a subject, identify and study related verses in their context, and one or more truths consistent with the verses will emerge. Sometimes I cannot see how to reconcile what appears to be conflicting verses, but in every case, with continued prayerful study, I have found that the problem was with my personal views or lack of knowledge. In this way, consistent answers can be discovered.

3. There must be a commitment to pursue the truth as revealed in the Bible without cultural, religious, or personal bias. I believe that, in some cases, selected Bible verses are used to support a point of view while other verses are ignored. This is the basis for some denominational differences.

4. In some cases, the truths revealed are clear; in others, there is partial revelation. Some of the subjects in the Bible, like the creation of the world, predestination, and the atoning death of Christ, cannot be completely understood and thus remain as mysteries beyond human understanding. However, the Bible does reveal sufficient details on these and other mysteries that show God's plan and purpose for our lives.

5. The meaning of scriptures as discussed in this book is based solely on the New International Version (NIV). My objective is not to debate the merits of various translations. The NIV is a widely used

---

3   In reply Jesus declared, "I tell you the truth, no one can see the kingdom of God unless he is born again."(Jn 3:3)
     But when he, the Spirit of Truth, comes, he will guide you into all truth. He will not speak on his own: he will speak only what he hears, and he will tell you what is yet to come. (Jn 16:13)

and understandable translation. I will leave it to Bible scholars to argue the most accurate translations to the English language.

The Bible says that those who are perishing (going to hell), consider it to be nonsense or incomprehensible, while those who are saved find it to be a source of truth and life.[4] How can this be? The answer lies in the most profound and precious experience that there is in this life: a spiritual birth.

Humans are creatures comprised of body, mind, and spirit.[5] Humans are living in a world that is influenced by forces of good and evil. The presence of evil in and around us has resulted in a broken relationship with God. Man has not always been in this broken relationship with God as can be seen with Adam and Eve's relationship with God before they chose to experience evil. God walked and talked with them.[6] It was after they sinned that their experience of God and knowledge of God was diminished and they were driven from the Garden of Eden.[7]

This diminished knowledge and experience of God grew as mankind chose to experience different types of evil. The result is that mankind has become separated from God and does not understand or even seek after Him.[8] Indeed, we have all sinned, offended God, and are headed for eternal punishment and separation from Him.[9]

---

4   For the message of the cross is foolishness to those who are perishing, but to us who are being saved it is the power of God. (1Cor 1:18)

5   May God himself, the God of peace, sanctify you through and through. May your whole spirit, soul, and body be kept blameless at the coming of our Lord Jesus Christ. (1Th 5:23)

6   Then the man and his wife heard the sound of the Lord God as he was walking in the garden in the cool of the day, and they hid from the Lord God among the trees of the garden. (Gn 3:8)

7   So the Lord God banished him from the Garden of Eden to work the ground from which he had been taken. (Gn 3:23)

8   there is no one who understands, no one who seeks God. (Rom 3:11)

9   for all have sinned and fall short of the glory of God. (Rom 3:23)

Fortunately, God has taken the initiative to restore a relationship with him. Because he is a higher being and is the offended party, restoration is on his terms. The Bible says in Hebrews 9:22 that forgiveness of sins requires the shedding of blood (death penalty). God made it possible for mankind to be restored through the death of Jesus Christ upon the cross. Jesus offered himself as a substitute for the death penalty we all deserve because of our sins. When he completed this work, he said, "It is finished."[10] Man cannot add or subtract from it. Each person must decide whether to believe and receive it by faith.[11] Jesus said "I am the way, the truth and the life, no man can come to the Father (God) except by me."[12]

Jesus said that unless a man is born again he cannot see the kingdom of God. How is this accomplished? It is by believing you are a sinner and that Jesus died for your sins, and by calling upon Jesus to be your savior.[13] It is by this earnest plea of faith in Jesus Christ alone that it is possible to become a child of God and experience a spiritual birth. Good deeds cannot restore our relationship with God.[14]

What then is the role of religion and good works? The answer to this and many other common questions are found in this book.

---

10   When he had received the drink, Jesus said, "It is finished." With that, he
      bowed his head and gave up his spirit. (Jn 19:30)

11   Jesus answered, "I am the way and the truth and the life. No one comes to
      the Father except through me." (Jn 14:6)

12   Jesus answered, "I am the way and the truth and the life. No one comes to
      the Father except through me." (Jn 14:6)

13   But God demonstrates his own love for us in this: While we were yet
      sinners, Christ died for us. (Rom 5:8)
      And everyone who calls on the name of the Lord will be saved. (Acts 2:21)

14   For it is by grace you have been saved, through faith—and this not from
      yourselves, it is the gift of God—not by works, so that no one can boast.
      (Eph 2:8-9)

Cited Abbreviations

Isaiah . . . . Isa
Daniel . . . . Da
Micah . . . . Mic
Nahum . . . . Na
Matthew . . . . Mt
Mark . . . . Mk
Luke . . . . Lk
John . . . . Jn
Acts . . . . Ac
Romans . . . . Ro
1 Corinthians 1Co
2 Corinthians 2Co
Galatians . . . . Gal
Ephesians . . . . Eph
Philippians . . . . Php
Colossians . . . . Col
1 Thessalonians 1Th
2 Thessalonians 2Th
1 Timothy 1Ti
2 Timothy 2Ti
Titus . . . . Tit
Hebrews . . . . Heb
James . . . . Jas
Jude . . . . Jude
1 Peter 1Pe
2 Peter 2Pe
1 John 1Jn
2 John 2Jn
Revelation . . . . Rev

A Full and Meaningful Life

Life is full of routines like sleeping, eating, and working, with occasional milestones such as marriage, birth, and death. Seasons and years come and go. Even special events like vacations and holidays can become repetitious, less exciting, and less meaningful as we grow older. So how can we live a full and meaningful life?

There are three common approaches that consume most of our time, talents, and energy. One approach is the pursuit of material things. Americans are in love with having a modern home, late model cars, lots of clothes, a wide variety of food, and as many new electronic gadgets as possible. The desire for more and better things has resulted in a throwaway society where new is better, savings are low, and debt is high. The cost and quantity of things that are accumulated measure success.

There are two problems with the pursuit of material things. First, possessions tend to possess the possessor. The more you have, the more there is to take care of and worry about. I think about this whenever I cut and fertilize the lawn, wash the cars, and clean the house. Things break down and this is a continuing source of headaches and frustration.

Second, things and wealth that are accumulated are left behind when death occurs. Therefore, others benefit from your hard work to accumulate things. This can be good or bad depending on whether the inheritors are appreciative and wise in using the wealth passed on to them. The bottom line is that man enters this world with nothing and takes nothing out of it, so it is not true that the one who dies with the most things, wins.

The second popular philosophy of life is the pursuit of pleasures to experience life to the fullest. This results in a lifestyle that seeks self-gratification through traveling, multiple sexual partners, drugs, new restaurants, new electronic gadgets and entertainment forms seeking excitement and pleasures that are fleeting. There is no lasting satisfaction in this approach and it leads to frustration. Most people do not have enough time or money to experience all the possible places, people, food and things that life has to offer. Indeed, even if it were possible to have unlimited wealth, there would always be places and things beyond our experience due to the limits of the human life span.

A full life cannot be measured by the quantity, but rather by the quality of one's relationships with others and with God. The Apostle Paul, after having been beaten, ship-wrecked and thrown into prison, wrote that he had lived a full life and was content in whatever situation he found himself.[15] Paul said that as long as he had Jesus, he could do anything through the strength of God's presence and power.[16]

A third popular pursuit is to leave a legacy. Living for family, fame, or fortune may be noble, but it is ultimately futile. Family members and human relationships seldom turn out the way we like.

---

15   I know what it is to be in need, and I know what it is to have plenty. I have learned the secret of being content in any and every situation, whether well fed or hungry, whether living in plenty or in want. (Php 4:11-12)

16   I can do everything through him who gives me strength. (Php 4:13)

Fame and fortune dwindle over time, and facts are frequently altered to meet political, cultural, or religious objectives. King Solomon was among the most powerful and wealthy rulers of his day. During his rule, the kingdom of Israel reached its largest expanse and many surrounding kings paid tribute to him. His reputation for wisdom spread far and wide and prompted the Queen of Sheba to travel to see him.[17] He had vast wealth and wisdom. He tried all of life's pursuits but, in the end, found them all to be meaningless vanity like he was chasing after the wind.[18] He concluded that the best that man could hope for was to find satisfaction in labor, do good works, and fear God.[19] This is the best that man can hope for without a saving relationship with Jesus, who said that abundant and meaningful life comes from knowing him as one's personal savior.[20]

---

17 She said to the king, "The report I heard in my own country about your achievements and your wisdom is true. But I did not believe these things until I came and saw with my own eyes. Indeed, not even half was told me; in wisdom and wealth you have far exceeded the report I heard. (1 Ki 10:6-7)

18 I devoted my-self to study and to explore by wisdom all that is done under heaven. What a heavy burden God has laid on men? I have seen all the things that are done under the sun; all of them are meaningless, a chasing after the wind. (Ecc 1:13-14)

19 I know that there is nothing better for men to be happy and do good while they live. That everyone may eat and drink, and find satisfaction in all his toil—this is the gift of God. (Ecc 3:12-13)

20 I am the gate; whoever enters through me will be saved. He will come in and go out, and find pasture. The thief comes only to steal and kill and destroy; I have come that they may have life, and have it to the full. (Jn 10:9-10)

Discussion Questions

1. What would your first impulse be if you had unlimited money?

2. After careful thought and prayer, what should you do if you had unlimited money?

3. What is the difference between your first impulse (i.e. would) and your second choice (i.e. should)?

4. Have you ever thought or prayed something like "Dear God, if you would somehow make it possible for me to have a lot of money, I promise to give $$$$ to the poor." Do you think this is trying to bribe God?

5. Do you think that winning the lottery or inheriting millions of dollars would tend to make you closer or further from God? Why?

6. What is your idea of a full life?

7. What is your idea of a meaningful life?

8. What is God's idea of a full and meaningful life?
(Jn 10:9-10; Jn 5:30; Dt 6:5)

9. Americans from lower-income families tend to give a higher percentage of their income to charity than middle- or high-income families. What are some of the reasons for this?

10. How would your life be different if you started to make changes based on the following priorities listed below?

a) Develop a mission statement that summarizes what is most important to you.

b) Give of your talents, time or money to causes that align with your mission statement.

c) People are more important than a schedule so you must be giving and flexible to show that completing tasks is secondary to building relationships.

d) Discover and set priorities around family activities that are meaningful and important rather than duties or traditions.

e) Be willing to make changes in life rather than trusting in fate.

f) Find value in the daily routines of life rather than take them for granted or think of them as something to be endured so that you can get to a better routine.

Abortion

There are no words in the Bible that translate to the equivalent of abortion. However, the murder of humans is prohibited by the Ten Commandments.[21] There are many different Greek and Hebrew words in the Bible that are translated to mean kill, slay, or murder. In Numbers 31:17, God commands the Israelites to kill some of the conquered Midianites. Obviously, there must be a difference in these commands, since, by his very nature, God cannot contradict himself.

This can be resolved by viewing the prohibition on killing as murder in which the act is premeditated and is for personal (usually selfish) reasons. The killing referred to in Numbers 31:17 and elsewhere, commanded by God to the Israelites, refers to the execution of evil people by a government or nation. God bestowed

---

21   You shall not murder. (Dt 5:17)

upon governments the right to kill as a penalty for crimes and to maintain social order.[22]

The preceding discussion is relevant to abortion since it is clearly a premeditated act on the part of the mother that ends the life of her offspring. Common reasons for having an abortion are generally selfish such as: "It's my body," or "I can't afford or don't want the baby." Therefore, abortion qualifies as murder except in circumstances beyond the control of the mother, such as medical complications that threaten the life of the mother. Some argue that a fetus is not human and so abortion is not murder, but merely the surgical removal of unwanted foreign tissue growing inside the mother. Very few would argue that life does not begin at conception. What is argued is whether or when the fetus is human.

The Bible says that only God gives life, and he therefore has the right to take it.[23] In Isaiah 45:9-10, God likens himself to a potter and humans to clay worked into pots. God says that man (the clay) has no right to question what God (the potter) has created and is developing in the womb. God knows and forms each of us while we are still in the womb.[24] He not only knows and forms us in the womb, but he also has plans for us. God desires for us to fulfill some

---

22   And for your lifeblood I will surely demand an accounting. I will demand an accounting from every animal. And from each man, too, I will demand an accounting for the life of his fellow man. Whoever sheds the blood of man, by man shall his blood be shed; for in the image of God has God made man. (Ge 9:5-6)

23   Now listen, you who say, "Today or tomorrow we will go to this or that city, spend a year there, carry on business and make money." Why, you do not even know what will happen tomorrow. What is your life? You are a mist that appears for a little while and then vanishes. Instead, you ought to say, "If it is the Lord's will, we will live and do this or that." (Jas 4:13-15)

24   This is what the Lord says—he who made you, who formed you in the womb, and who will help you. (Isa 44:2)

unique purpose of his, which may or may not be clearly known to us in this life.[25]

Children are a blessing from God.[26] It is clear from the Bible that God gives life, knows us, and has plans for each of us even before we are born. To end God's plans and purposes through abortion is to use the free will that God has given us to usurp his sovereignty. This is rebellion, which is the root of all sins.

---

25   My frame was not hidden from you when I was made in the secret place. When I was woven together in the depths of the earth, your eyes saw my unformed body. All the days ordained for me were written in your book before one of them came to be. (Ps 139:15-16)

26   Sons are like a heritage from the Lord, children a reward from him. (Ps 127:3)

Discussion Questions

1. What are some of the reasons why abortion remains legal in America?

2. Why do women in America have abortions?

3. Do you think that testing the amniotic fluid or other such tests for birth defects affects abortion decisions? Should it?

4. Do you think that sexual themes in movies and television and abortions are related?

5. Do you think there is a relationship between abortions and rising concerns over human population growth, rising expectations in living standards and global environmentalism?

6. Is there any comfort or hope for those who have had an abortion?

7. Do you think that rape or incest is a valid reason for having an abortion?

8. What are some of the possible emotions felt by women who have had abortions? Do you think there are similarities in feelings with women who have had miscarriages? Why or why not?

9. What are some reasons why abortion rates tend to be higher in developing countries?

10. What are some reasons that explain why, in the United States, most of the women who have abortions are in their twenties and have never been married?

11. How do you view birth control as a means of reducing abortions?

12. Some forms of birth control such as the pill, RU-486 (morning after pill) and intra-uterine devices are designed to keep the embryo from implanting in the uterus. Does your view of these methods differ from your view of more natural methods such as rhythm or conception barriers?

Am I A Christian?

Over thirty years ago I prayed to receive Jesus Christ as my personal Savior and Lord. Soon afterwards, I heard a nagging voice in my head tell me "It isn't that easy to get to heaven" and "You are fooling yourself if you think God can readily and easily forgive you for all the wrongs you have done." I have also seen those who struggle with this question and go forward many times in church to accept Christ or try to prove by their good works that there has been a genuine change. So how can a person know for sure that a spiritual birth has occurred, that sins have been forgiven and that they are a new creation indwelt by the Holy Spirit?[27]

The Bible says in 2 Corinthians 13:5 "examine yourselves to see whether you are in the faith; test yourselves. Do you not realize that Christ Jesus is in you unless, of course, you fail the test?" From this we see that each person must examine themselves about whether they have been transformed into a child of God by faith in Jesus. Nobody can do this for you or assure you that it has happened within

---

27   Yet to all who received him, to those who believed in his name, he gave the right to become children of God--children born not of natural descent nor of human decision or a husband's will, but born of God. (Jn 1:12-13)

you. Only you can answer this question. What are the questions we should be asking to evaluate this important change? I recently taught a Sunday School Class on this subject and we compiled a list of questions to do this self-examination. These questions are not listed in any order of importance.

Do I have a hunger or spiritual craving for the Word of God?

The words of the Bible are inspired by the Holy Spirit and thus are God's words.[28] Therefore, this is a way to be connected with God and results in spiritual growth in knowledge, transformation and equipping for doing good works. There should be a need or hunger to read, meditate and memorize the Bible. This is more than a regular discipline of reading. It is a driving desire that should result in reading the Bible very often. How often do you eat? Reading the Bible should be nourishment to the soul as food is to the body.

Do you pray regularly?

Prayer is conversation with God. For those who are born again, this happens both consciously and unconsciously. The latter occurs continuously because born again believers have been transformed into temples where the presence Holy Spirit dwells.[29] The Holy Spirit constantly prays for us.[30] On the conscious level, prayers

---

28 All Scripture is God-breathed and is useful for teaching, rebuking, correcting and training in righteousness, so that the man of God may be thoroughly equipped for every good work. (2 Ti 3:16)

29 Do you not know that your body is a temple of the Holy Spirit, who is in you, whom you have received from God? (1Cor 6:19)

30 In the same way, the Spirit helps us in our weakness. We do not know what we ought to pray for, but the Spirit himself intercedes for us with groans that words cannot express. (Ro 8:26)

may be private or communal but should be more than a routine or discipline. Prayer for the genuine believer is conversation, worship and praise directed to the most precious being in life. Therefore, do you pray only when you need something or as part of a routine such as meals, church or bedtime? There is nothing wrong with these types of prayers but even those of other religions do these things. For the child of God, prayer can include these things but is much more. Prayer is an ever increasing preoccupation with God that transforms the mind resulting in a heightened awareness of His presence, purpose and power.[31]

Do you desire to spend time with other believers and love them?

"Birds of a feather flock together" is a good analogy. If you are born again, you will desire to associate with those of like mind and spirit. The presence of the Holy Spirit in others is a powerful attracting force that draws believers together and unifies them despite personality, cultural, racial, ethnic or any other differences. The person of the Holy Spirit is the life of God in us and is a foundation upon which believers are transformed.[32] Above all else, it is the love of God in us and the love we have for other believers that is a characteristic of born again believers.[33]

---

31 Be joyful always, pray continually, give thanks in all circumstances, for this is God's will for you in Christ Jesus. (1Th 5:16-18)

32 And we, who with unveiled faces all reflect the Lord's glory, are being transformed into his likeness with ever-increasing glory, which comes from the Lord, who is the Spirit. (2Co 3:18)

33 "A new command I give you: Love one another. As I have loved you, so you must love one another. By this all men will know that you are my disciples, if you love one another." (Jn 13:34-35)

Do you have spiritual fruit and is it increasing in your life?

The indwelling Holy Spirit transforms our minds resulting in character and life-style changes. The presence of the Holy Spirit causes permanent, irreversible and progressive changes in each believer making the following qualities grow: love, joy, peace, patience, kindness, goodness, gentleness and self- control.[34]

Do you desire to share your faith in Jesus with others?

If you have been born again, you will be filled with the love, joy and peace resulting from the presence of the Holy Spirit within. This experience is so wonderful that you will desire to share it with others. You will want to tell others about how this change happened to you both to see if others have also been born again and in the hope that others may also experience this birth. Jesus commands his disciples to go and bear witness to who he is and his teachings.[35] The light and life of God within his children will shine forth if there has been a genuine birth.[36]

---

34   But the fruit of the Spirit is love, joy, peace, patience, kindness, goodness, faithfulness, gentleness and self-control. (Gal 5:22-23)

35   Then Jesus came to them and said, "All authority in heaven and on earth has been given to me. Therefore, go and make disciples of all nations, baptizing them in the name of the Father and of the Son and of the Holy Spirit, and teaching them to obey everything I have commanded you. And surely I am with you always, to the very end of the age." (Mt 28:18-20)

36   "You are the light of the world. A city on a hill cannot be hidden. Neither do people light a lamp and put it under a bowl. Instead they put it on its stand, and it gives light to everyone in the house. In the same way, let your light shine before men, that they may see your good deeds and praise your Father in heaven." (Mt 5:14-16)

Are you becoming more dependent upon God?

As time passes the presence of the Holy Spirit within transforms the mind so that priorities, thoughts and actions are increasingly centered on Jesus.[37] This results in a growing dependency upon God and the realization that he is the essence of life. Everything else seems secondary to his love (sensing the closeness of his presence), his purpose (pleasing him) and his power (sovereignty) and the revelation of truth (knowledge).[38]

Are you pursuing holiness?

As children of God, we are commanded to be holy as God is holy.[39] This does not mean that holiness can be achieved through human effort but rather that holiness grows inside true believers and manifests itself in good works as the mind is transformed.[40] Are you

---

37 Therefore, I urge you, brothers, in view of God's mercy, to offer your bodies as living sacrifices, holy and pleasing to God—this is your spiritual act of worship. Do not conform any longer to the pattern of this world, but be transformed by the renewing of your mind. Then you will be able to test and approve what God's will is—his good, pleasing and perfect will. (Ro 12:1-2)

38 What is more, I consider everything a loss compared to the surpassing greatness of knowing Christ Jesus my Lord, for whose sake I have lost all things. (Php 3:8)

39 As obedient children, do not conform to the evil desires you had when you lived in ignorance. But just as he who called you is holy, so be holy in all you do; for it is written: "Be holy, because I am holy." (1Pe 1:14-16)

40 For we know that our old self was crucified with him so that the body of sin might be done away with, that we should no longer be slaves to sin—because anyone who has died has been freed from sin. (Ro 6:6-7)
    You have been set free from sin and have become slaves to righteousness. I put this in human terms because you are weak in your natural selves. Just as you used to offer the parts of your body in slavery to impurity and to ever-increasing wickedness, so now offer them in slavery to righteousness leading to holiness. (Ro 6:18-19)

doing good works to show you are a Christian (do to be) or do your good works flow from who you are (be to do)?

Is God disciplining you? Do you feel the unrest of sin in your life?

There should be a growing awareness of sin within and around the true believer. This results in a sense of the greatness of our sinful condition and a desire to be rid of sinful habits. Paul describes the tension of true believers who experience conflict between the desires of the Holy Spirit and human nature.[41] This unrest is part of the conviction of the Holy Spirit who is working to overcome the evil nature. True believers are more miserable than others after sinning because choosing sin breaks fellowship with God and results in his displeasure and discipline.[42]

These are some of the questions that each person should use to see if there has been a spiritual birth into the kingdom of God. Jesus said that no man can enter the kingdom of God unless the Holy Spirit causes him to be born in a spiritual sense as a new creation.[43] Do you pass these tests?

---

41 So I find this law at work: When I want to do good, evil is right there with me. For in my inner being I delight in God's law, but I see another law at work in the members of my body, waging war against the law of my mind and making me a prisoner of the law of sin at work within my members. (Ro 7:21-23)

42 My son, do not despise the Lord's discipline and do not resent his rebuke, because the Lord disciplines those he loves, as a father the son he delights in. (Pr 3:11-12)

43 In reply Jesus declared, "I tell you the truth, no one can see the kingdom of God unless he is born again." (Jn 3:3)

Discussion Questions

1. Why does the Bible challenge us to examine ourselves to be certain that we have genuine faith in Jesus?

2. Are self-examinations uncomfortable? If so, why?

3. Discuss why humans are more comfortable with having the church help to define us through sacraments and rituals.

4. What is the proper role of sacraments and rituals?

5. Do you think that a born again Christian has more conflict within and with those outside the church than someone who professes to be a Christian and lives like everyone else the rest of the week?

6. Discuss how your perspective of right and wrong has changed since you were born again.

7. How have your relationships with those closest to you been affected since your spiritual birth?

8. Has your thinking changed since your spiritual birth? How has this affected your actions?

Angels

Angels are a higher life form than humans and thus have wisdom and powers beyond human understanding. When Jesus entered the world as a baby, the Bible says that he was made a little lower than the angels.[44] Angels are called God's mighty ones who do his bidding.[45] An angel shut the mouths of lions so that they would not harm Daniel.[46] One hundred and eighty-five thousand Assyrian soldiers were killed in one night by an angel.[47] These are some examples of why angels are much more powerful than humans.

It appears that all angels were created at one time and no new angels are being added to the number. Angels are not subject to

---

44   But we see Jesus, who was made a little lower than the angels, now crowned with glory and honor because he suffered death, so that by the grace of God he might taste death for everyone. (Heb 2:9)

45   Praise the Lord, you his angels, you mighty ones who do his bidding. (Ps 103:20)

46   My God sent his angel and he shut the mouths of the lions. They have not hurt me, because I was found innocent in his sight. Nor have I ever done any wrong before you, O king. (Da 6:22)

47   That night the angel of the Lord went out and put to death a hundred and eighty-five thousand men in the Assyrian camp. When the people got up the next morning—there were all the dead bodies! (2Ki 19:35)

death or any form of extinction; therefore they do not decrease in number. Angels in the Bible never appear as cute, chubby infants. They are always full-grown adults. The response of people who see angels as told in the Bible is typically fear and awe.

There are different ranks or levels of authority and duties among angels. Those called seraphs attend the throne of God and lead in praise and worship.[48] Another rank or type of angel is the cherub, whose members also surround the throne of God.[49] The Bible mentions angels of commander rank called archangels, who lead other angels. Revelation 12:7 describes a war between the archangel Michael leading the angels of heaven, and the devil and his fallen angels or demons. Michael the archangel is called one of the chief princes of God's faithful angels.[50]

Angels are associated with churches, places, and people, perhaps related to their rank and power. Revelation 1:20 speaks of the seven angels assigned to the Christian churches named in chapters 2 and 3. Michael the archangel is associated with Israel, while an evil angel who opposes him in Daniel 10:21, is called the Prince of Persia (modern-day Iran).

---

48   In the year that King Uzziah died, I saw the Lord seated on a throne, high and exalted, and the train of his robe filled the temple. Above him were seraphs, each with six wings: With two wings they covered their faces, with two they covered their feet, and with two they were flying. And they were calling to one another: "Holy, holy, holy is the Lord Almighty; the whole earth is full of his glory." (Isa 6:1-3)

49   And Hezekiah prayed to the Lord: "O Lord, God of Israel, enthroned between the cherubim, you alone are God over all the kingdoms of the earth. You have made heaven and earth." (2Ki 19:15)

50   But the prince of the Persian kingdom resisted me twenty-one days. Then Michael, one of the chief princes, came to help me, because I was detained there with the king of Persia. (Da 10:13)

God's angels perform many acts of service. They will separate mankind into good and evil groups destined for heaven or hell.[51] Revelation chapter 16 says that angels shall dispense the wrath and judgments of God upon unbelievers during the tribulation. The angel Gabriel appeared to the Virgin Mary and announced that she would be the mother of Jesus.[52] A multitude of angels announced the birth of Jesus to shepherds.[53] Angels carried messages from God to man in the dreams of Joseph, warning him of Herod's plans to kill the infant Jesus.[54] An angel was present at the tomb of Jesus and announced his

---

51   The field is the world, and the good seed stands for the sons of the kingdom. The weeds are the sons of the evil one, and the enemy who sows them is the devil. The harvest is the end of the age, and the harvesters are angels. As the weeds are pulled up and burned in the fire, so it will be at the end of the age. The Son of Man will send out his angels, and they will weed out of his kingdom everything that causes sin and all who do evil. They will throw them into the fiery furnace, where there will be weeping and gnashing of teeth. Then the righteous will shine like the sun in the kingdom of their Father. He who has ears, let him hear. (Mt 13:38-43)

52   In the sixth month, God sent the angel Gabriel to Nazareth, a town in Galilee, to a virgin pledged to be married to a man named Joseph, a descendant of David. The virgin's name was Mary. The angel went to her and said, "Greetings, you who are highly favored! The Lord is with you." (Lk 1:26-28)

53   An angel of the Lord appeared to them, and the glory of the Lord shone around them, and they were terrified. But the angel said to them, "Do not be afraid. I bring you good news of great joy that will be for all the people. Today in the town of David a Savior has been born to you; he is Christ the Lord. This will be a sign to you: You will find a baby wrapped in cloths and lying in a manger." (Lk 2:9-12)

54   But after he had considered this, an angel of the Lord appeared to him in a dream and said, "Joseph, son of David, do not be afraid to take Mary home as your wife, because what is conceived in her is from the Holy Spirit." (Mt 1:20)

resurrection.[55] The Israelites were guided by an angel from Egypt to the Promised Land.[56] Angels attended Jesus after his encounter with the devil in the desert.[57]

Angels act as commanded by God and their actions are sometimes in response to the prayers of believers. Peter was freed from prison by an angel.[58] This angel suddenly appeared between two guards in the cell where Peter was in chains. God apparently gave this angel orders in response to believers' prayers for Peter. In Daniel 10:12-13, an angel is sent by God to Daniel in response to his prayers and fasting. However, the appearance of the angel to Daniel with God's message was delayed because one or more evil angels opposed him.

According to the Bible, angels are assigned to those who will become believers from the time they are infants.[59] Angels protect

---

55   There was a violent earthquake, for an angel of the Lord came down from heaven and, going to the tomb, rolled back the stone and sat on it. His appearance was like lightning, and his clothes were white as snow. The guards were so afraid of him that they shook and became like dead men. The angel said to the women, "Do not be afraid, for I know that you are looking for Jesus, who was crucified. He is not here; he has risen, just as he said. Come and see the place where he lay. (Mt 28:2-6)

56   but when we cried out to the Lord, he heard our cry and sent an angel and brought us out of Egypt. (Nu 20:16)

57   Then the devil left him, and angels came and attended him. (Mt 4:11)

58   So Peter was kept in prison, but the church was earnestly praying to God for him. The night before Herod was to bring him to trial, Peter was sleeping between two soldiers, bound with two chains, and sentries stood guard at the entrance. Suddenly an angel of the Lord appeared and a light shone in the cell. He struck Peter on the side and woke him up. "Quick, get up!" he said, and the chains fell off Peter's wrists. (Ac 12:5-7)

59   Are not all angels ministering spirits sent to serve those who will inherit salvation? (Heb 1:14)
     See that you do not look down on one of these little ones. For I tell you that their angels in heaven always see the face of my Father in heaven. (Mt 18:10)

those they are assigned to.[60] After death, angels accompany and guide those God has forgiven of their sins.[61]

Angels are primarily spirit beings but sometimes take human form. Genesis 19 records the visit of two angels in the form of men to the city of Sodom. Also, in Genesis chapter 18, three angels in the form of men visited Abraham and Sarah in their old age to announce the birth of Isaac. The Greek and Hebrew words for angel are masculine in gender, but sex in the human sense is not associated with angels.[62]

In the Old Testament, the term "Angel of the Lord" refers to God in many cases where he spoke or appeared to different prophets and leaders. In Genesis 22:15, the Angel of the Lord calls to Abraham from heaven. In Exodus 3:2, the Angel of the Lord speaks to Moses from the burning bush. The Angel of the Lord brought the Israelites out of Egypt to the Promised Land.[63]

Evil angels or demons are those who chose to follow the cherub Lucifer in rebelling against God.[64] One-third of the angels chose to

---

60   For he will command his angels concerning you to guard you in all your ways; (Ps 91:11)
The angel of the Lord encamps around those who fear him, and he delivers them. (Ps 34:7)

61   The time came when the beggar died and the angels carried him to Abraham's side. The rich man also died and was buried. (Lk 16:22)

62   At the resurrection people will neither marry nor be given in marriage; they will be like the angels in heaven. (Mt 22:30)

63   The angel of the Lord went up from Gilgal to Bokim and said, "I brought you up out of Egypt and led you into the land that I swore to give to your forefathers. I said, 'I will never break my covenant with you, (Jdg 2:1)

64   How you have fallen from heaven, O morning star, son of the dawn! You have been cast down to the earth, you who once laid low the nations! You said in your heart, "I will ascend to heaven; I will raise my throne above the stars of God; I will sit enthroned on the mount of assembly, on the utmost heights of the sacred mountain. I will ascend above the tops of the clouds; I will make myself like the Most High." But you are brought down to the grave, to the depths of the pit. (Isa 14:12-15)

rebel against God, lost their places in heaven and were cast to the earth.[65] Some of these fallen angels are bound in darkness awaiting judgment.[66] Others are able to roam the earth with the devil until the final judgment, when they will be cast into hell.[67]

---

65   And the angels who did not keep their positions of authority but abandoned their own home—these he has kept in darkness, bound with everlasting chains for judgment on the great Day. (Jude 6)

66   For if God did not spare angels when they sinned, but sent them to hell, putting them into gloomy dungeons to be held for judgment; (2Pe 2:4)

67   And the devil, who deceived them, was thrown into the lake of burning sulfur, where the beast and the false prophet had been thrown. They will be tormented day and night forever and ever. (Rev 20:10)

Discussion Questions

1. The Bible warns against becoming too pre-occupied with angels. Why do you think there is a natural fascination about angels?

2. Have you ever had an experience that you would attribute to guardian angels?

3. Have you ever seen, sensed or experienced the presence of angels or demons?

4. Did you know that born again Christians will someday judge angels? Read 1 Corinthians 6:3.

5. When you think of angels, what images come to mind? Why? Are these images Biblical? How do these images compare with the seraphs described in Isaiah 6:1-3?

6. Angels are mentioned at least 108 times in the Old Testament and 165 times in the New Testament. Does this tell you anything about the presence of angels in our world?

Anxiety (Worry)

Life is full of many concerns stemming from the absence of certainty and control of our future. While we can never be completely free from worry, the Bible shows us how to minimize it in our lives.

In Philippians 4:6-7 Paul advises us to not worry about anything. Instead, he tells us to pray about our needs and include thanking God for answering past prayers. Believers are commanded to pray about life's worries. These prayers are to be more than requests for favorable answers. They are to include thanksgiving and praise along with the needs. Praying in this way reminds us of the many blessings God continually gives us whether or not we ask for them. This reminds us of God's great love for us and that he knows us and does what is best for us.

Worry is proportional to our sense of security. When life is going as planned and we feel safe in our life routines, then worries subside. Likewise worry increases when we feel threatened and insecure or are overly focused on and committed to some result. First Peter 5:7 says that we should cast our cares upon Jesus because he cares for us. The recommended practice for believers is to take our worries to Jesus in prayer and leave them with him. This reinforces our dependence on, and faith in, Jesus.

Worries increase when we become focused on the things of this world. Jesus said the treasures of this world are subject to decay and can be taken away, but heavenly treasures are secure.[68] Therefore, we should set our priorities on God and not on money.[69] Man worries about such things as having food and clothes but is given life by God. God provides life without which the concerns of life are meaningless. Worry can cause ulcers and mental problems that can have destructive health effects that shorten life. No amount of worry will add even one hour to one's life.[70] Therefore, why worry? The Bible teaches that we should deal with each day's problems when they occur and not be obsessed with future concerns that may not happen.[71]

In Luke 10:38-42, Jesus visits the house of the sisters Martha and Mary. Martha was busy with many details regarding making Jesus and his disciples comfortable. Mary, on the other hand, was sitting at the feet of Jesus listening to what he said. Martha complained to Jesus that Mary should be busy helping, but Jesus told Martha that "…you are worried and anxious about many things, but only one thing is needed. Mary has chosen what is better and it will not be taken away from her."[72]

---

68   Do not store up for yourselves treasures on earth, where moth and rust destroy, and where thieves break in and steal. (Mt 6:19)

69   No one can serve two masters. Either he will hate the one and love the other, or he will be devoted to the one and despise the other. You cannot serve both God and Money. (Mt 6:24)

70   Who of you by worrying can add a single hour to his life? (Mt 6:27)

71   Therefore do not worry about tomorrow, for tomorrow will worry about itself. Each day has enough trouble of its own. (Mt 6:34)

72   "Martha, Martha," the Lord answered, "you are worried and upset about many things, but only one thing is needed. Mary has chosen what is better, and it will not be taken away from her."(Lk 10:41-42)

What is this one thing that freed Mary from the busyness and worries experienced by her sister? Mary chose to focus on Jesus, listen to him, and ignore the immediate demands of hospitality. I do not believe that Mary was being irresponsible; rather, she wanted to experience and learn from Jesus first, and later, when he was done speaking, she would fulfill her duties. Mary had her priorities straight. Put God first and he will free us from worries and take care of the rest of our concerns. Worry is a warning signal that we have pushed God out of the driver seat and we are trying to navigate based on our own efforts.

Discussion Questions

1. What do you worry about the most? Make a list and compare the similarities or differences with others.

2. Do the worries at the top of your list reflect what is most important to you?

3. How do you deal with worry? How should we deal with it?

4. Is worry ever a good thing? If so, list some positive outcomes or responses.

5. Read Philippians 4:6-8. We are told not to worry but to pray with thanksgiving and present our requests to God. Why is thanksgiving an important part of eliminating worry?

6. In Matthew 6:34, Jesus tells us to focus on the challenges of each day and not those of the future. Why? Does this mean that we are not to plan for the future? What is the difference between planning for the future and worrying about it?

7. Do you think that worry stems from wishful thinking? If so, do you see a problem with The Lord's Prayer and wishful thinking?

8. Chronic worry can cause physical illnesses such as heart attacks, high blood pressure, ulcers, gastrointestinal problems, muscular aches and pains and skin rashes. How does this happen? What does this tell you about the importance of the thought life?

9. Worry is self-talk in which we tell ourselves something, usually on a repeating basis that often distracts the mind from focusing on the present. Have you ever been distracted by worries while driving or doing something until you had a near miss or cut yourself while preparing food?

10. Do you think that there is a genetic tendency to worry that runs in families?

11. Do you think that children who experience one or more divorces of their parents are more likely to be chronic worriers?

12. Do you worry more about the future, present or past? Why?

Appearance

There are limited verses that speak to the subject of appropriate physical appearance. The Bible teaches that women should dress modestly and that beauty is not to be measured by outward adornment, but by one's character.[73]

Men and women must not dress in clothing such that they appear to be of the opposite sex. Men are not to have long hair because it is a feminine trait.[74] How long can a man's hair be before it is too long? The Bible is silent on this level of detail, and so it is a matter of personal conscience. In the Old Testament, Samson had long hair and those under an oath to God (i.e. Nazarites) did not cut their hair as a sign of their dedication. However, men who strive to

---

73   I also want women to dress modestly, with decency and propriety, not with braided hair or gold or pearls or expensive clothes (1Ti 2:9)

74   Does not the very nature of things teach you that if a man has long hair, it is a disgrace to him, but that if a woman has long hair, it is her glory? For long hair is given to her as a covering. (1Co 11:14-15)

be effeminate are called wicked in God's view.[75] Finally, making any cuttings in the body, including tattoos, is forbidden by God.[76]

---

75   Do you not know that the wicked will not inherit the kingdom of God? Do not be deceived: Neither the sexually immoral nor idolaters nor adulterers nor male prostitutes nor homosexual offenders nor thieves nor slanderers nor swindlers will inherit the kingdom of God. (1 Co 6:9-10)

76   Do not cut your bodies for the dead or put tattoo marks on yourselves. I am the Lord. (Lev 19:28)

Discussion Questions

1. List some good and evil men in the Bible and in various cultures that had long hair, such as Absalom, Beethoven, Einstein and The Beatles. Did their hair length make a statement about themselves or was it considered customary in that time and place?

2. In 1 Peter 3:3-4, believers are urged to focus on the development of inner rather than outer beauty. Why? Is there a problem with seeking beauty through clothing and makeup?

3. Name some popular people who have tattoos. What kind of personality traits do they portray by having many tattoos?

4. What are some of the common shapes, patterns, messages and images used in tattoos that come to mind?

5. What are some popular places on the body that people have tattoos? Why is this?

6. A 2008 Harris Poll found that 14% of all adults in America had at least one tattoo. The highest incidence of tattoos was found among the gay, lesbian and bisexual population (25%), among Americans ages 25 to 29 years (32%) and those ages 30 to 39 years (25%). Why do you think that these groups tend to have more tattoos?

7. Those with tattoos said that having a tattoo made them feel more rebellious (36%), while others said a tattoo made them feel more sexy (31%). Do the placement and types of tattoos you have seen support these views?[77]

---

77   *The Vanishing Tatoo, Facts & Statistics*, Harris Poll #15, February 12, 2008, http://www.vanishingtattoo.com/tattoo_facts.htm#Harris_Poll

Baptism

Baptism is one of two ordinances that Jesus gave to believers, the other being communion. Unlike communion, which is to be practiced regularly, baptism is generally held to be a one-time event in the life of every believer. Sometimes baptism is performed twice if infant baptism is performed and later the person is born again and is baptized as a testimony to their spiritual birth by faith. While there are no explicit examples of infant baptism in the Bible, there are cases where entire households were baptized.[78] In such cases, it is possible that infants may also have been baptized. In some Christian denominations, infant baptism is performed as the New Testament

---

78   When she and the members of her household were baptized, she invited us
      to her home. (Acts 16:15)
      At that hour of the night the jailer took them and washed their wounds,
      then immediately he and all his family were baptized. (Acts 16:33)

equivalent of circumcision in the Old Testament: as a sign of God's covenant with Abraham.[79]

Jesus commanded the apostles to make disciples of all men and baptize them.[80] Water symbolizes baptism and so is a physical representation of the spiritual attributes of the person baptized.[81] There are several things that happen to a person being baptized that portray spiritual truths. First, let's examine what things can be observed during baptism:

- There is physical contact and interaction of the person with the water.
- The water penetrates and permeates the body surfaces it touches.
- There is some degree of co-mingling of the water with body fluids.
- There is a cleansing action of the water.
- The person is transformed in appearance by contact with the water.

The Bible says that believers in Christ experience a spiritual birth in which there is contact and interaction between the spirit of the believer and the Holy Spirit of God. I believe this is the baptism of the Holy Spirit referred to in Acts 1:5; 11:15-16 and Matthew 3:11. Baptism is a physical representation of this spiritual contact, interaction, and birth process. There is adequate support in the Bible to say that this aspect of baptism is a re-enactment of a saving,

---

79 I will establish my covenant as an everlasting covenant between me and your descendants after you for the generations to come, to be your God and the God of your descendants after you. (Ge 17:7)
This is my covenant with you and your descendants after you, the covenant you are to keep: Every male among you shall be circumcised. You are to undergo circumcision, and it will be the sign of the covenant between me and you. (Ge 17:10-11)

80 Therefore go and make disciples of all nations, baptizing them in the name of the Father and of the Son and of the Holy Spirit, (Mt 28:19)

81 and this water symbolizes baptism that now saves you also—not the removal of dirt from the body but the pledge of a good conscience toward God. It saves you by the resurrection of Jesus Christ, (1Pe 3:21)

spiritual birth that has been experienced previously and not at the time of the water baptism. Evidence for this is seen in the conversion of the Ethiopian eunuch by Philip in Acts 8:35-38, in which the eunuch believes and is baptized. This is also the order of events supported by the conversions of various persons recorded in Acts 2:41; 8:12-13; and 16:31-33 where faith precedes water baptism.

The washing or cleansing aspect is described in Titus 3:5-6, in which Paul says that a person is born spiritually "...through the washing of rebirth and renewal by the Holy Spirit whom he (God) poured out on us generously through Jesus Christ our Savior." The idea of God's Holy Spirit being poured generously upon the believer during spiritual rebirth is recalled in the drenching action of water during baptism.

In the Bible, the word baptism is sometimes used to describe the act of identifying with someone or something. Examples of this are seen in 1 Corinthians 1:13 and 10:2, where persons are described as being baptized into Paul or Moses. Other verses refer to baptism as a picture of death and resurrection.[82] This is illustrated in the baptism ceremony when the believer is immersed (i.e. buried) in the water and emerges transformed, which is a picture of the future promise of a new resurrected body and life.

I believe Jesus was baptized to identify with sinners. Those who were being baptized by John were doing so as a sign of their sorrow and repentance for their sins.[83] The identification of God the Father and the Holy Spirit with Jesus as the Messiah are also seen

---

82   We were therefore buried with him through baptism into death in order that, just as Christ was raised from the dead through the glory of the Father, we too may live a new life. (Ro 6:4)
      having been buried with him in baptism and raised with him through your faith in the power of God, who raised him from the dead. (Col 2:12)

83   I baptize you with water for repentance. But after me will come one who is more powerful than I, whose sandals I am not fit to carry. He will baptize you with the Holy Spirit and with fire. (Mt 3:11)

in Matthew 3:16-17. Jesus began the phase of his life in which he proclaimed himself as Messiah with his baptism. Likewise, born again believers are commanded to proclaim their spiritual birth and identify with Jesus as Savior and Lord through baptism.[84]

Baptism is not essential for salvation, as is evident from many verses in the Bible.[85] Baptism is a wonderful way to express love for Jesus as Savior and to be obedient to him as Lord. It is a way to symbolically express one's spiritual birth and to identify with Jesus. It is an important public milestone that proclaims the fact of a spiritual birth. It is typically a one-time event for believers and so should be a personal decision in response to the leading of the Holy Spirit. When experienced this way, baptism can be a very exhilarating experience. Just as wedding vows are sometimes repeated, I believe that believers should not be prohibited or dissuaded from periodically repeating the baptism ordinance to express love, gratitude, and unity with Jesus.

---

84   Peter replied, "Repent and be baptized, every one of you, in the name of Jesus Christ for the forgiveness of your sins. And you will receive the gift of the Holy Spirit." (Acts 2:38)

85   That if you confess with your mouth, "Jesus is Lord," and believe in your heart that God raised him from the dead, you will be saved. For it is with your heart that you believe and are justified, and it is with your mouth that you confess and are saved. (Ro 10:9-10)

Discussion Questions

1. Name the different practices and beliefs about baptism that are prevalent among Christians. Why do you think that beliefs about baptism have become a common way that denominations distinguish themselves from others?

2. While baptism is not required for salvation, it is an important way to make a public profession of faith in Jesus. Can you think of any Bible verses that support the idea that true believers in Jesus will bear witness to him as Savior and Lord?

3. What makes infant baptism an attractive idea from the view of the parents and relatives?

4. How does infant baptism differ from dedications performed in some churches?

5. In Mt 3:11, John the Baptist talks about being baptized by water as a sign of repentance. He says that the Messiah will baptize with the Holy Spirit and fire. What do you think this means? Do you think that this baptism will be simultaneous or sequential regarding baptism by the Holy Spirit and fire?

6. The earliest usual form of baptism among early Christians was for the candidate to be immersed. A later form, for which there is pictorial evidence from the 3rd century onwards, was to have the candidate stand in water while water was poured over their upper

body. Other common forms of baptism now in use include pouring water three times on the forehead. What do you think are some of the motivating reasons for such variations in baptism?

7. Infant baptism is believed to have originated around 400 AD when the theologian Augustine taught it as a solution for "original sin." This idea is that humans inherit the sin of Adam at birth and are separated from God from the beginning of life. This sinful state caused concerns among parents who feared for their children if they died before they had the opportunity to "get right with God." This fear led to the practice of infant baptism being performed to remove original sin.[86] This implies that baptism alone is sufficient for salvation. What do you think of this? Find Bible verses to support your views.

---

86   *Clarifying Christianity, What is Baptism?* http://www.clarifyingchristianity. com/get_wet.shtml

Communion

Communion is one of two ordinances that Jesus gave to believers, the other being baptism, as mentioned earlier. Unlike baptism, which is typically a one-time event in the life of a Christian, communion is to be repeated throughout the life of each believer.[87]

The term "communion" is used to describe this ordinance today; it is not found in the Bible. So what is communion? The word "communion" suggests a common or communal union. Some aspects are clearly described in the Bible, while others are metaphorical, mystical, and cannot be completely defined or understood. First, let's examine what is clearly stated.

The components of communion, bread and wine, are reminders of the body and blood sacrifice of Jesus on the cross.[88] Even more than this, taking communion is a public (and private) identification

---

87　They devoted themselves to the apostles' teaching and to the fellowship, to the breaking of bread and to prayer. (Ac 2:42)

88　And he took bread, gave thanks and broke it, and gave it to them, saying, "This is my body given for you; do this in remembrance of me." In the same way, after the supper he took the cup, saying, "This is my blood, which is poured out for you." (Lk 22:19-20)

with Christ as savior and a proclamation of faith in his return.[89] There are mystical aspects to communion as well. It is important to prepare mentally prior to taking communion to be sure that the sacrifice of Jesus is discerned and appreciated.[90] If communion is taken in an unworthy manner, there will be grave consequences. Paul says God will judge those who do not take communion properly and that our relationship with God will become weak and damaged.

What does it mean to take communion properly? In 1 Corinthians 11:27-28, Paul says that it is necessary to recognize the body and blood of Jesus when taking communion. Therefore, it is important to come to the communion table with humility and gratitude. The bread and wine are physical emblems of Christ's broken body and his blood poured out as a peace offering for those who have accepted this as the exclusive means of satisfying the wrath of God caused by our sins. The Bible says that without the shedding of blood, there is no forgiveness of sins and that the penalty for sin is death.[91] Jesus satisfied these conditions through his death on the cross for those who accept this sacrifice as their own. Believers become part of an action by Jesus in one point in time that transcends time in that it enables people throughout time to be called forgiven and

---

89   For whenever you eat this bread and drink this cup, you proclaim the Lord's death until he comes. (1Co 11:26)

90   Therefore, whoever eats the bread or drinks the cup of the Lord in an unworthy manner will be guilty of sinning against the body and blood of the Lord. A man ought to examine himself before he eats of the bread and drinks of the cup. For anyone who eats and drinks without recognizing the body of the Lord, eats and drinks judgment on himself. (1Co 11:27-29)

91   In fact, the law requires that nearly everything be cleansed with blood, and without the shedding of blood there is no forgiveness. (Heb 9:22) For the wages of sin is death, but the gift of God is eternal life in Jesus Christ our Lord. (Ro 6:23)

worthy to be in the presence of God.[92] Therefore, in a spiritual sense, believers were with Jesus when he made atonement for sins. This is why Paul says he is crucified with Christ (in a spiritual and positional sense), nevertheless he lives, but in a new condition with the spirit of Christ indwelling, renewing and guiding him in a transformed life.[93] Communion symbolizes the hope believers have for righteousness and a restored relationship with God through Jesus Christ.

Taking communion is a reminder of the great love of Jesus and the great cost he was willing to pay to provide a future perfect relationship with those who believe in him.[94] Communion should fill every believer with gratitude, awe, hope, humility, and wonder at the great lengths that Jesus took in leaving heaven to take the form of a carpenter's son, to live the life we could not, and experience death on behalf of all mankind! Communion is a celebration of the love relationship made possible by the sacrifice of Jesus that is both intimately personal and communal.

There is much more to communion that defies description and must be experienced. I will attempt to describe some of the metaphorical and mystical aspects as I have experienced them. Communion has nurturing, strengthening, encouraging, and identifying aspects. It abounds with symbolism that describes some of its mystical qualities. Bread is a basic food that sustains physical

---

92   Therefore, brothers, since we have confidence to enter the Most Holy Place by the blood of Jesus, by a new and living way opened for us through the curtain, that is, his body, and since we have a great priest over the house of God, let us draw near to God with a sincere heart in full assurance of faith, having our hearts sprinkled to cleanse us from a guilty conscience and having our bodies washed with pure water. (Heb 10:19-22)

93   I am crucified with Christ and I no longer live, but Christ lives in me. The life I live in the body, I live by faith in the Son of God, who loved me and gave himself for me. (Gal 2:20)

94   Let us fix our eyes on Jesus, the author and perfecter of our faith, who for the joy set before him endured the cross, scorning its shame, and sat down at the right hand of the throne of God. (Heb 12:2)

life. I believe Jesus chose this food to teach that he gives and sustains the spiritual life of believers. Jesus identifies his body with the bread of communion.[95] The breaking of bread during communion is a picture of the broken body of Jesus. During communion, large pieces of bread are generally broken into smaller ones that are consumed by the participants. This is a picture of how Jesus enters into the core of each believer and, just as the bread is digested and becomes part of the body, so does Jesus become one with each believer.

This also is an illustration of the unity of believers in Jesus Christ. The same bread becomes transformed into many believers who are nourished by the same physical bread. Jesus said he is the spiritual bread that gives life to those who come to him and believe in him.[96] The spiritual parallel is that believers share the presence of the Holy Spirit and are transformed by accepting the broken body of Jesus as a sacrifice for their sins. Bread not only sustains, but it also strengthens the body to do work. Likewise, communion strengthens, encourages, and deepens devotion to Jesus, increasing resolve to serve him.

The wine also has similar symbolic elements of unity, intimacy, and transformation. In addition, the wine is associated with the blood of Christ, which covers the sins of believers. Wine marks or stains what it contacts and is symbolic of the fact that believers have been marked by the presence of the Holy Spirit. Wine also has cleansing and healing connotations, which are reminders of the sin atonement of Christ's blood.

---

95   While they were eating, Jesus took bread, gave thanks and broke it, and gave it to his disciples saying, "Take it; this is my body." (Mk 14:22)

96   Then Jesus declared, "I am the bread of life. He who comes to me will never go hungry, and he who believes in me will never be thirsty." (Jn 6:35)

Communion is a celebration of the presence of Christ in believers, with the focus being the awesome love and goodness of Jesus in redeeming and transforming those who accept his sacrifice for their sins. It is a unique and intensely personal way to encounter God, and thus believers are encouraged to participate regularly!

Discussion Questions

1. List some adjectives that describe what thoughts and emotions you have experienced when taking communion. Do you see some common themes?

2. The name communion suggests communal union. Discuss the ways that communion is a picture of physical, emotional and spiritual unity.

3. In most churches, the prevailing mood during communion is sad because the focus is on the torture and death Jesus had to endure because of sin. Do you think this is unbalanced behavior? Should there be a joyful component to celebrating communion? What might be some reasons for this view?

4. How often do you participate in communion? Is this the right frequency for you? What are some pros and cons related to daily communion?

5. The teachings about communion vary among Christian denominations from a purely memorial and symbolic sacrament to literally partaking of the very body and blood of Christ. Where do these differences come from? Find Bible references to support the various views.

Eating and Drinking

Some Christian churches in America demonize drinking any alcohol while encouraging (or at least remaining silent on) excessive eating. The Bible clearly says that drunkenness is a sin. Ephesians 5:18 says, "Do not get drunk on wine which leads to debauchery" (bad behavior). Also, 1 Corinthians 6:9-10 says, "Do not be deceived: neither the sexually immoral nor idolaters nor adulterers nor male prostitutes nor homosexuals nor thieves nor the greedy nor drunkards...will inherit the Kingdom of God."

There is no prohibition, however, against drinking alcoholic beverages. In fact, Jesus said that it is not what enters the body through the mouth (eating and drinking) that makes a person unclean.[97] The Bible also says that what a person does or does not eat or drink does not make one pleasing to God but rather it is having righteousness, peace, and joy in the Holy Spirit, which results from being born again into the Kingdom of God.[98]

---

97   What goes into a man's mouth does not make him "unclean" but what comes out of his mouth that is what makes him "unclean." (Mt 15:11)

98   For the kingdom of God is not a matter of eating and drinking, but of righteousness, peace and joy in the Holy Spirit, (Ro14:17)

The story of how Jesus changed water into wine at the Canaan wedding feast recorded in John 2:1-10 does not make sense unless the wine that Jesus changed from water was fermented. In verse 10, the steward tastes the wine made from water and says that, at most marriage feasts, the best wine is served first, and after the guests have drunk freely, the cheaper wine is served. This custom would make sense only if the wine was fermented as the ability of the guests to discern the difference would be diminished by the alcohol. In this case, the steward says that the wine from water should have been served first as it was better.

Bible verses that suggest that drinking wine is good, such as 1 Timothy 5:23, are many times explained away by saying that the use of the word wine is a translation problem and what is really referred to is grape juice. This does not make sense given the verses previously mentioned plus favorable references to wine found in Psalms 104:15 and Song of Songs 1:2. Sometimes, the prohibition against drinking any fermented wine by Nazarites is taken as evidence against consuming any alcoholic beverages.[99] However, these verses also say that a Nazarite is not to eat grapes or raisins. I have never heard of any church that says eating grapes or raisins is a sin. Furthermore, in Numbers 6:20, the Bible says that a person taking the vow of a Nazarite may again drink wine once the period of the vow is completed.

It is reasonable to infer from Luke 1:15 and Mat 27:34 that Jesus did not take wine or other fermented drinks. However, there is evidence that Jesus was part of social gatherings where alcohol was

---

99   Speak to the Israelites and say to them: "If a man or woman wants to
      make a special vow, a vow of separation to the Lord as a Nazirite, he must
      abstain from wine and other fermented drink and must not drink vinegar
      made from wine or from other fermented drink. He must not drink grape
      juice or eat grapes or raisins. As long as he is a Nazirite, he must not eat
      anything that comes from the grapevine, not even the seeds or skins." (Nu
      6:2-4)

consumed, such as the Canaan wedding feast. Matthew 11:19 says that he was accused of being a glutton and drunkard because of his eating and drinking habits. Obviously, this is an exaggeration of the truth by those religious leaders who were seeking to discredit him. If this is an exaggeration of what Jesus did, this would not make sense unless Jesus was at least commonly found with those who did consume some alcohol.[100]

Proverbs 20:1 says that those who are overcome (i.e. become drunk) by alcohol are unwise, which is a warning to drink responsibly, not a complete prohibition. One of the qualifications of being a church leader or elder was that potential candidates must not be given to drunkenness.[101] Also, Paul instructs that older women who are believers should be a positive example by not overindulging in too much wine.[102] These verses indicate that self-control in the consumption of alcoholic drinks was Paul's message, not abstinence.

If it is OK to drink some alcoholic beverages, but not to be drunk, how much is acceptable? The Bible also provides guidance in this area. 1Timothy 5:23 says taking a little wine to drink is healthy. Proverbs 23:20 advises us to not associate or participate with those who drink to excess. Therefore, do not drink to the point where you

---

100   While Jesus was having dinner at Matthew's house, many tax collectors and "sinners" came and ate with him and his disciples. (Mt 9:10)

101   Since an overseer is entrusted with God's work, he must be blameless— not overbearing, not quick-tempered, not given to drunkenness, not violent, not pursuing dishonest gain. (Tit 1:7)
Now the overseer must be above reproach, the husband of but one wife, temperate, self-controlled, respectable, hospitable, able to teach, not given to drunkenness, not violent but gentle, not quarrelsome, not a lover of money. (1Ti 3:2-3)

102   Likewise, teach the older women to be reverent in the way they live, not to be slanderers or addicted to much wine, but to teach what is good. (Tit 2:3)

become dizzy.[103] I have found that I know when I have had enough just as my body tells me when I have eaten enough. Beyond this point, peer pressure or pride (to show others that I can handle it) is the reason to continue drinking and leads to drunkenness. The Bible says, if you do not have self-control, then do not drink.[104]

"All food is clean, but it is wrong for a man to eat anything that causes someone else to stumble. It is better not to eat meat or drink wine or do anything that causes your brother to fall."[105] Another principle is: if you drink, do not encourage others to do so to the point of drunkenness. Note that these verses say that we should encourage others to **not eat** as well as **not drink** to excess. The care of our bodies is part of our stewardship in serving God. We are to have a sound (or healthy) mind, body and spirit.[106] Exercise is encouraged.[107]

While many Christian churches teach that any consumption of alcohol is sinful, they generally are silent in the areas of eating and exercise. In fact, I have found that church potluck dinners tend to

---

103 Who has woe? Who has sorrow? Who has strife? Who has complaints? Who has needless bruises? Who has bloodshot eyes? Those who linger over wine, who go to sample bowls of mixed wine. Do not gaze at wine when it is red, when it sparkles in the cup, when it goes down smoothly! In the end it bites like a snake and poisons like a viper. Your eyes will see strange sights and your mind imagine confusing things. You will be like one sleeping on the high seas, lying on top of the rigging. (Pr 23:29-34)

104 If your hand or your foot causes you to sin, cut it off and throw it away. It is better to enter life maimed or crippled than to have two hands or two feet and be thrown into eternal fire. (Mt 18:8)

105 All food is clean, but it is wrong for a man to eat anything that causes someone else to stumble. It is better not to eat meat or drink wine or to do anything else that will cause your brother to fall. (Ro 14:20-21)

106 May God himself, the God of peace, sanctify you through and through. May your whole spirit, soul and body be kept blameless at the coming of our Lord Jesus Christ. (1Th 5:23)

107 For physical training is of some value, but godliness has value for all things, holding promise for both the present life and the life to come. (1Ti 4:8)

promote the consumption of more food than is normally eaten. There are seldom any admonitions to eat responsibly. On the contrary, the quality of the "fellowship" seems to focus on the abundance and indulgence in food.

While spiritual development (i.e. becoming more Christ like) and mental development (i.e. reading and memorizing the Bible) are encouraged, physical exercise is not. In fact, I have found that physical exercise is sometimes considered a waste of time or a worldly weakness pursued by those who do not have their priorities straight.

While I agree that it is not good to become obsessed with physical appearance, I believe that it is also wrong to ignore the importance of regular exercise. The Bible says that we are creatures with a mind, soul, and body. We are stewards accountable to God for all that we have and are. This includes keeping ourselves in good physical condition by reasonable eating and a disciplined exercise routine.

Discussion Questions

1. Many Christians would not enter a bar but readily go into restaurants that specialize in unlimited food bars. What is the difference between over-eating and drinking too much?

2. If a Christian is abstaining from eating meat during Lent or for some other reason and you are together in the restaurant, what should your response be?

3. There seems to be a lack of preaching or emphasis on the need to exercise and keep physically fit. Why is this? Do you think a lack of physical fitness hurts our witness for Christ?

4. Do you fast? If so, how often do you fast? Discuss what motivates you to fast. If you do not fast, why don't you?

5. Find passages in the New Testament on fasting. Is fasting an option for believers?

6. Alcoholism research performed by The National Center on Addiction and Substance Abuse (CASA) at Columbia University in 2005 found that 9.6% of adult alcoholics drink 25% of the alcohol that is consumed by all adult drinkers.[108] What are some of the reasons for heavy drinking?

---

108 *About Alcohol Facts, The National Center on Addiction and Substance Abuse (CASA) at Columbia University in 2005,* http://www.about-alcohol-facts. com/

7. Medical research has found greater longevity among men who drink moderately than among those who either abstain or drink heavily. Benefits include lowered risk of dementia, type-two diabetes and heart disease.[109] What effects does alcohol have on the body that supports these findings?

109 *Alcoholism: Clinical & Experimental Research*, 6-14-04; Berman, Jessica. Moderate alcohol consumption benefits heart, U.S. government says. Voice of America News, 6-16-04, http://www2.potsdam.edu/hansondj/ InTheNews/MedicalReports/Longevity/1088617919.html

Faith That Works

The role of faith and works in salvation is a topic that has been and continues to be debated among Christians. Clearly, faith and good works are related and without works faith is dead or useless.[110] There are a number of paradoxes in the Bible associated with faith and works that would disappear if Christians would realize that it is who they are that should drive what they do. In other words, "be to do" not "do to be." Our human thinking and culture tells us we need to work hard to gain skills and knowledge to be successful and attain a better way of life. This is "do to be" thinking. I believe this thinking has pervaded Christianity such that the motivation to do good works, receive the sacraments, achieve status and rank by becoming a priest, deacon, elder, etc. is based on the desire to accumulate spiritual rewards and a better place in heaven. Another problem is that some Christian denominations teach that works are an essential part of salvation. In other words, the grace needed

---

110 You foolish man, do you want evidence that faith without deeds is useless? Was not our ancestor Abraham considered righteous for what he did when he offered his son Isaac on the altar? You see that his faith and his actions were working together, and his faith was made complete by what he did. (Jas 2:20-22)

to reach heaven is imparted through the sacraments of the church which again is "do to be" thinking.

So what is "be to do" Christian thinking? The basis for this thinking rests on a spiritual birth through faith in Jesus Christ as personal savior.[111] Jesus said that one must be born again in order to enter the kingdom of God.[112] The death of Jesus on the cross provides payment for the penalty of the sins of mankind. This is a legal transaction that enables those who accept this by faith to become children of God indwelt by the Holy Spirit.[113] This spiritual birth is like the natural one in that growth in knowledge of the new identity of self, the presence and guidance of the Holy Spirit and the works that result are progressive. From this theological view, good works are a result of changes that God has produced inside me and not changes that I try to achieve by doing something. Thus, the meaning of Jesus in saying that in order to gain life you must lose it means that you must be born again or changed spiritually through faith in Jesus.[114] When this happens there is a fundamental change in self- identity in which a person's thinking shifts from "me" to "we" as a result of the presence of the Holy Spirit. In my case, I began to

---

111   "For God so loved the world that he gave his one and only Son, that whoever believes in him shall not perish but have eternal life. (Jn 3:16) For it is by grace you have been saved, through faith—and this not from yourselves, it is the gift of God—not by works, so that on one can boast. (Eph 2:8-9)

112   In reply Jesus said, "I tell you the truth, no one can see the kingdom of God unless he is born again."

113   For the wages of sin is death, but the gift of God is eternal life in Christ Jesus our Lord. (Ro 6:23)
       You are all sons of God through faith in Christ Jesus. (Gal 3:26)
       Don't you know that you yourselves are God's temple and that God's Spirit lives in you? (1Co3:16)

114   "Whosoever tries to keep his life will lose it, and whoever loses his life will preserve it." (Lk 17:33)

live for Jesus and not just for myself so, in this way, I have lost my life but found new life and joy in serving Jesus.

Likewise, faith without works is dead means that there can be no genuine change within (i.e. spiritual birth in Jesus) without changes in outward actions. The outward actions or good works result from the reality of spiritual changes within and not visa- versa. Thus, the greatest in the kingdom of God are servants or slaves who, like Jesus, follow the will of God. What they do is a result of what God has already done within them. Good works becomes an expression of love, gratitude and obedience that desires to give God joy. The result of such good works is a deeper experience of the presence of God within. I fear that too many Christian denominations stress works because they are led by human understanding and a desire to self-improve or control others rather than as a result of being fundamentally changed by a spiritual birth.

Discussion Questions

1. Many Christian denominations have a progression of sacraments such as baptism, communion, confirmation, etc. that follow the progression of life. Discuss pros and cons of this related to faith and works.

2. Discuss "do to be" thinking and how this type of thinking is reinforced through our educational and business systems.

3. Is "be to do" thinking unnatural? Why is it difficult when it comes to Christian living?

4. Is it possible to deceive ourselves and others by pretending to "be" someone other than who we really are?

5. If we pretend to "be" someone other than who we are for an extended period of time, how does this affect our happiness and our state of mind?

6. Thinking drives behavior. Discuss how the presence of the Holy Spirit changes thinking and values.

7. If who we are and what we do result from changes that God brings about within us, what is our role in doing good works?

8. How are good works, heavenly rewards, our transformation to holiness and our relationship with God related?

Forgiveness

"To error is human but to forgive is divine." (Alexander Pope). Humans are prone to sin and make mistakes, and so there are none without sin in God's eyes.[115] God is gracious and is willing to forgive provided men repent.[116] Sins, errors, and offenses *may* involve other humans but *always* involve God.

David had an affair with Bathsheba, who was another man's wife. He tried to cover up this affair by lying, arranged for her husband to be killed, and then married her. When David repented of these things, he realized that the primary offenses were against God, even though his actions were directed at humans.[117]

There can be no forgiveness unless the one offended is willing to accept the transgressor despite what has been done. God has a

---

115   for all have sinned and fall short of the glory of God (Ro 3:23)

116   The Lord is not slow in keeping his promise, as some understand slowness. He is patient with you, not wanting anyone to perish, but everyone to come to repentance. (2Pe 3:9)

117   Against you, you only, have I sinned and done what is evil in your sight so that you are proved right when you speak and justified when you judge. (Ps 51:4)

merciful nature and desires to forgive because he loves.[118] However, his holiness demands that there be restitution or payment of a penalty. The penalty for sin is death, but the good news is that God has paid the penalty through the death of Jesus.[119]

When God forgives, he chooses not to think about the offenses and they are blotted out or removed from the record of transgressions subject to judgment.[120] In effect, those forgiven are forever changed in God's eyes and become new creatures, children of light and heirs of heaven.[121] "Blessed are they whose transgressions are forgiven, whose sins are covered. Blessed is the man whose sin the Lord will never count against him."[122]

---

118   You are forgiving and good, O Lord, abounding in love to all who call to you. (Ps 86:5)
      You are forgiving and good, O Lord, abounding in love to all who call to you. (Ps 86:5)

119   For the wages of sin is death, but the gift of God is eternal life in Christ Jesus our Lord. (Ro 6:23)
      In fact, the law requires that nearly everything be cleansed with blood and without the shedding of blood there is no forgiveness. (Heb 9:22)

120   as far as the east is from the west, so far has he removed our transgressions from us. (Ps 103:12)
      No longer will a man teach his neighbor, or a man his brother, saying, "Know the Lord," because they will all know me, from the least of them to the greatest, declares the Lord. For I will forgive their wickedness and will remember their sins no more. (Jer 31:34)

121   Therefore, if anyone is in Christ, his is a new creation; the old has gone, the new has come! (Eph 5:8) For you were once in darkness, but now you are light in the Lord. Live as children of the light. (2Co 5:17)
      God and co-heirs with Christ, if indeed we share in his sufferings in order that we may also share in his glory. (Ro 8:17)

122   Blessed are they whose transgressions are forgiven, whose sins are covered. Blessed is the man whose sin the Lord will never count against him.(Ro 4:7-8)

God's forgiveness is not based on anything that can be done by man to obligate or persuade God to do it.[123] God chooses whom he wills to forgive based on his own purposes and graciousness.[124] This is why God says "...I will have mercy on whom I will have mercy and I will have compassion on whom I will have compassion."[125] This is why Jesus spoke in parables, because it is only to the elect of God that the experience of spiritual birth, the revelation of God in the heart, and the renewal of the mind are realized.[126]

The Bible says that believers have been forgiven of their sins and reconciled to God. Therefore, they are to forgive others and be ambassadors of reconciliation.[127] God is displeased with believers who do not forgive others and will judge and punish those who refuse to do so.[128] Jesus taught that there are to be no limits to the

---

123 For it is by grace you have been saved, through faith—and this not from yourselves, it is the gift of God—not by works, so that no one can boast. (Eph 2:8-9)

124 who has saved us and called us to a holy life—not because of anything we have done but because of his own purpose and grace. This grace was given us in Christ Jesus before the beginning of time. (2Ti 1:9)

125 And the Lord said, "I will cause all my goodness to pass in front of you, and I will proclaim my name, the Lord, in your presence. I will have mercy on whom I will have mercy, and I will have compassion on whom I will have compassion. (Ex 33:19)

126 He told them, "The secret of the kingdom of God has been given to you. But to those on the outside everything is said in parables so that, 'they may be ever seeing but never perceiving, and ever hearing but never understanding; otherwise they might turn and be forgiven!'" (Mk 4:11-12)

127 All this is from God, who reconciled us to himself through Christ and gave us the ministry of reconciliation: that God was reconciling the world to himself in Christ, not counting men's sins against them. And he has committed to us the message of reconciliation. We are therefore Christ's ambassadors, as though God were making his appeal through us. We implore you on Christ's behalf; be reconciled to God. (2Co 5:18-20)

128 For if you forgive men when they sin against you, your heavenly Father will also forgive you. But if you do not forgive men their sins, your Father will not forgive your sins. (Mt 6:14-15)

number of times believers are to forgive others.[129] God's kindness and compassion remind believers to forgive.[130] Refusal to forgive others sets oneself above everything else, resulting in selfishness and self-righteousness. This is shown in the parable of the wicked servant who was punished by his master for refusing to forgive a minor debt, when he had been forgiven much.[131] We must forgive each other if we expect to be forgiven by God.[132]

---

129 Then Peter came to Jesus and asked, "Lord, how many times shall I forgive my brother when he sins against me? Up to seven times?" Jesus answered, "I tell you not seven times, but seventy-seven times." (Mt 18:21-22)

130 All this is from God, who reconciled us to himself through Christ and gave us the ministry of reconciliation: that God was reconciling the world to himself in Christ, not counting men's sins against them. And he has committed to us the message of reconciliation. We are therefore Christ's ambassadors, as though God were making his appeal through us. We implore you on Christ's behalf; be reconciled to God. (2Co 5:18-20)

131 Therefore, the kingdom of heaven is like a king who wanted to settle accounts with his servants. As he began the settlement, a man who owed him ten thousand talents was brought to him. Since he was not able to pay, the master ordered that he and his wife and his children and all that he had be sold to repay the debt. The servant fell on his knees before him. "Be patient with me," he begged, "and I will pay back everything." The servant's master took pity on him, canceled the debt and let him go. But when that servant went out, he found one of his fellow servants who owed him a hundred denarii. He grabbed him and began to choke him. "Pay back what you owe me!" he demanded. His fellow servant fell to his knees and begged him, "Be patient with me, and I will pay you back." But he refused. Instead, he went off and had the man thrown into prison until he could pay the debt. When the other servants saw what had happened, they were greatly distressed and went and told their master everything that had happened. Then the master called the servant in. "You wicked servant," he said, "I canceled all that debt of yours because you begged me to. Shouldn't you have had mercy on your fellow servant just as I had on you?" In anger his master turned him over to the jailers to be tortured, until he should pay back all he owed. This is how my heavenly Father will treat each of you unless you forgive your brother from your heart. (Mt 18:23-35)

132 For if you forgive men when they sin against you, your heavenly Father will also forgive you. But if you do not forgive men their sins, your Father will not forgive your sins. (Mt 6:14-15)

Failure to forgive others multiplies troubles within ourselves and results in damaged relationships. Loneliness, depression, and distress are the results of failure to forgive others. Conversely, forgiveness restores relationships and affirms love and acceptance, avoiding rejection and the resulting sorrows and regrets.[133]

Because of God's provision of forgiveness through faith in Jesus, believers respond with eternal praise and honor to God. Believers have experienced the joy of his presence and relief from the penalty of their sins.[134]

God is willing to forgive every type of sin except for blasphemy against the Holy Spirit.[135] Jesus said that forgiveness will never be extended to those who commit this sin.[136] A parallel passage is found in Mark 3:28-29. In both places, Jesus responds to religious leaders who rejected him and attributed the miracles he performed to the power of the devil. To reject the spiritual manifestation of God in the works of the Holy Spirit in the life of Jesus made it impossible for forgiveness to occur. Those whose hearts are blind to the presence and prompting of the Holy Spirit can never be saved. Forgiveness begins with the recognition of sinfulness and the need to seek it, prompted by the Holy Spirit.

---

133 If anyone has caused grief, he has not so much grieved me as he has grieved all of you, to some extent—not to put it too severely. The punishment inflicted on him by the majority is sufficient for him. Now instead, you ought to forgive and comfort him, so that he will not be overwhelmed by excessive sorrow. I urge you, therefore, to reaffirm your love for him. (2Co 2:5-8)

134 And they sang a new song: "You are worthy to take the scroll and to open its seals, because you were slain, and with your blood you purchased men for God from every tribe and language and people and nation. You have made them to be a kingdom and priests to serve our God, and they will reign on the earth." (Rev 5:9-10)

135 And so I tell you, every sin and blasphemy will be forgiven men, but the blasphemy against the Spirit will not be forgiven. (Mt 12:31)

136 Anyone who speaks a word against the Son of Man will be forgiven, but anyone who speaks against the Holy Spirit will not be forgiven, either in this age or in the age to come. (Mt 12:32)

Discussion Questions

1. "Forgive and forget" is a popular saying. What does this mean? Is it possible to do this?

2. Why is it hard to forgive others? List reasons and discuss.

3. What occurs to relationships when there is no forgiveness?

4. Are there eternal consequences if we do not forgive others? (Mt 6:14-15)

5. Forgive and you shall be free. Withhold forgiveness and you hold yourself in bondage to the emotions and thoughts that keep you from being free. Do you agree?

6. Jesus said that real forgiveness is a matter of the heart and not just words. (Mt 18:35) What are some internal changes that happen when forgiveness comes from the heart?

7. Is there a difference between repentance and saying you are sorry? Why is repentance tied to forgiveness by God? (Ac 17:30; Lk 13:3; 2Co 7:10)

8. In Ephesians 4:30-31, Paul instructs believers to get rid of every form of malice against each other and to forgive others as Christ had forgiven them. In light of these verses, what character traits should be evident among believers?

9. Forgiveness unleashes joy. It brings peace. It washes the slate clean. It sets all the highest values of love in motion. In a sense, forgiveness is Christianity at its highest level. (John MacArthur)[137] Think of a time that you were forgiven of an offense you did to someone else. What emotions did you feel? What emotions did you feel when you forgave someone else for something they did to you?

137 *The Forgiveness Web, Forgiveness Quotations,* http://www.forgivenessweb. com/RdgRm/Quotationpage.html

Fortune Telling

People are naturally curious and anxious about the future. We live in the present with no guarantee or control over tomorrow. This state has led some to seek out people who claim to have special wisdom, insight, or powers, such as palm readers, psychics, magicians, enchanters, sorcerers, witches, and astrologers. The Bible maintains that these people are either frauds or they are in touch with evil spirits.

Acts 16:16-18 tells of a slave girl who was possessed by an evil spirit that enabled her to predict the future. God detests any form of fortune telling such as divination, interpreting omens, consulting the dead or acting as a medium for evil spirits.[138] Seeking to know and control future events is a form of rebellion against God's sovereignty. Proverbs 3:5-6 says that we are to trust completely in the Lord and

---

138 When you enter the land the Lord your God is giving you, do not learn to imitate the detestable ways of the nations there. Let no one be found among you who sacrifices his son or daughter in the fire, who practices divination or sorcery, interprets omens, engages in witchcraft, or casts spells, or who is a medium or spiritist or who consults the dead. Anyone who does these things is detestable to the Lord, and because of these detestable practices the Lord your God will drive out the nations before you. (Dt 18:9-12)

not on our own understanding. In everything we are to acknowledge him and trust him to direct our future. We are told to pray to God whenever there are worries regarding anything in the future.[139]

Those who consult mediums or spiritists defile themselves.[140] The Israelites were commanded to kill anyone who practiced witchcraft or was a medium or spiritist.[141] The nation of Israel was destroyed because the people chose to follow the evil practices of the surrounding peoples rather than obey God's commands.[142] God was provoked to anger against King Manasseh because he consulted mediums (i.e. witches) and spiritists.[143] King Saul consulted a witch or medium prior to his death in battle instead of turning to God in prayer.[144]

In the Old Testament, the Israelites consulted the high priest in major decisions where God's will was sought. The high priest wore a breastplate of stones called the Urim and Thummim through

---

139 Do not be anxious about anything, but in everything, by prayer and petition, with thanksgiving, present your requests to God. And the peace of God, which transcends all understanding, will guard your hearts and your minds in Christ Jesus. (Php 4:6-7)

140 Do not turn to mediums or seek out spiritists, for you will be defiled by them. I am the Lord your God. (Lev 19:31)

141 Do not allow a sorceress to live. (Ex 22:18)
A man or woman who is a spiritist among you must be put to death. You are to stone them; their blood will be on their own heads. (Lev 20:27)

142 Keep all my decrees and laws and follow them, so that the land where I am bringing you to live may not vomit you out. You must not live according to the customs of the nations I am going to drive out before you. Because they did all these things, I abhorred them. But I said to you, "You will possess their land; I will give it to you as an inheritance, a land flowing with milk and honey." I am the Lord your God, who has set you apart from the nations. (Lev 20:22-24)

143 He sacrificed his sons in the fire in the Valley of Ben Hinnom, practiced sorcery, divination, and witchcraft, and consulted mediums and spiritists. He did much evil in the eyes of the Lord, provoking him to anger. (2Ch 33:6)

144 Saul then said to his attendants, "Find me a woman who is a medium, so I may go and inquire of her." "There is one in Endor," they said. (1Sa 28:7)

which God communicated his will (how this was done is not clear from scripture, but could be something like the stones changed colors or glowed). An example of this is seen in God's command to Moses that Joshua consult Eleazar the high priest through the use of this breastplate of stones concerning the movement of the nation of Israel.[145]

Isn't this practice of decision making by the priests of Israel in using the stones on the high priest's vestments a form of divination? There are two reasons why this practice is different from divination. First, this was a method designated by God to communicate his will in making important and difficult decisions that affected his chosen people. Today believers have the indwelling Holy Spirit, but in the times of the nation of Israel they relied on the priests and prophets to discern God's will. Therefore, this practice affirmed God's sovereignty rather than usurped it by seeking another higher power source (i.e. demons). Second, there is no indication in the Bible that this practice was used to tell fortunes or predict future events; rather it was used mainly to make decisions.

Galatians 5:19-21 lists witchcraft among those acts that are sinful and says that those who live this way will not go to heaven. In light of these warnings and commands, there is no doubt that actions such as the use of tarot cards or Ouija boards are detestable to God. Anyone who consults psychics, witches, or palm readers and other spiritists are rebelling against God, who is the only one who knows and controls the future.

---

145   So the Lord said to Moses, "Take Joshua son of Nun, a man in whom is the spirit, and lay your hand on him. Have him stand before Eleazar the priest and the entire assembly and commission him in their presence. Give him some of your authority so the whole Israelite community will obey him. He is to stand before Eleazar the priest, who will obtain decisions for him by inquiring of the Urim before the Lord. At his command the entire community of the Israelites will go out, and at his command they will come in." (Nu 27:18-21)

Discussion Questions

1. Some popular fortune telling methods that are taken seriously by some and treated like a fun pastime by others include horoscopes, fortune cookies and the crazy eight-ball game. Discuss how these are like or different from such things as fortune telling, palm reading and Ouija boards.

2. What are some reasons why people want to know about their future? Do you see any common themes? How do you deal with these worries? What is the proper way to deal with these worries?

3. What do you think of the practice of seeking God's will by randomly opening the Bible?

4. What do you think about the predictions of Nostradamus?

5. Among the more unusual methods used to tell the future are the following:[146]
Scarpomancy: Predict someone's future by studying their old shoes.
Tiromancy: Study the shape, holes, mold, and other features on a piece of cheese.
Scatomancy: Predict your future by studying your own poop. (Not to be confused with *spatulamancy*, the study of "skin, bones, and excrement.")

---

146   *Neatorama, Bizzare Fortune Telling Methods,* Alex Santoso, Tuesday, August 21, 2007, http://www.neatorama.com/2007/08/21/bizarre-fortune-telling-methods/

Haruspication: Study the guts of an animal, preferably a sacred one.

What does this list tell you about the extremes people are willing to go to in order to feel like they have some insight to the future?

6. How is the need for security related to fortune telling?

7. In what ways does fortune telling appeal to human sinful nature?

8. How is fortune telling a form of rebellion against God?

Gambling

I believe that gambling means to risk something of personal value in order to have a chance to gain another's things that are coveted by the gambler. This is different from the practice of casting of lots described in the Bible. In fact, there are no terms or practices in the Bible that are equivalent to today's gambling practices. However, there are many verses in the Bible that give insight into the morality of gambling. Before looking at some of these verses, let's clear up the confusion over what casting of lots means and how it is different from gambling.

Casting lots was a way of making decisions by using specially marked objects such as stones, sticks or bones, which were thrown on the ground. Then someone would figure out the meaning based on their distribution. Lots were used to divide land and other goods in a fair way that avoided disputes.[147] When the Israelites conquered

---

147 Casting the lot settles disputes and keeps strong opponents apart. (Pr 18:18)

Canaan, they distributed the land by lot.[148] The robe of Jesus was a seamless garment that the soldiers cast lots for in order to possess it.[149] Lots also were used to make decisions such as the selection of warriors, the replacement of Judas, and to identify a sinner.[150] Casting lots in the Bible is different from gambling in that there was no personal risk of losing something of value for a chance to gain someone else's valuables.

While the Bible does not discuss gambling as we know it, there are many verses that deal with the motivating factors behind the desire to gamble. First is the love of money. People gamble because they are willing to risk their money for a chance to get more money. Gamblers are focused on, and captivated and motivated by, the love of money. I have observed gamblers in casinos and have noticed that they are focused, tense, show little emotion, and appear unhappy except when winning a significant amount of money. First Timothy 6:10 says that the love of money is the root of all kinds of evil. This is not to say that money is inherently evil, but that many evil desires and actions such as envy, stealing, and cheating, are motivated by

---

148　The Lord said to Moses, "The land is to be allotted to them as an inheritance based on the number of names. To a larger group give a larger inheritance, and to a smaller group a smaller one; each is to receive its inheritance according to the number of those listed. Be sure that the land is distributed by lot. What each group inherits will be according to the names for its ancestral tribe. Each inheritance is to be distributed by lot among the larger and smaller groups." (Nu 26:52-56)

149　"Let's not tear it," they said to one another. "Let's decide by lot who will get it." This happened that the scripture might be fulfilled which said, "They divided my garments among them and cast lots for my clothing." (Jn 19:24)

150　But now this is what we'll do to Gibeah: We'll go up against it as the lot directs. (Jdg 20:9)
Then they cast lots, and the lot fell to Matthias; so he was added to the eleven apostles. (Acts 1:26)
Then they cast lots, and the lot fell to Matthias; so he was added to the eleven apostles. (Acts 1:26)

the love of money. The Bible teaches that we are to be content with what we have.[151]

Those who gamble generally do so with the hope of winning enough money to fulfill some dream. The idea is to risk money for a chance to quickly have what may take years or a lifetime to earn. This is contrary to the Bible, which says that those who work hard will be rewarded but those who chase fantasies are foolish.[152] Laziness is behind the desire to get rich quick without working. The Bible says that laziness is a sin and leads to poverty.[153] The motivation to gamble is based on greed. It is the desire to have abundant wealth to gratify personal fantasies. The Bible warns against greed and the pursuit of abundant possessions.[154] Greed arises from covetousness which is an insatiable desire to have more. Covetousness is a sin and is addressed by one of the Ten Commandments.[155]

Gambling is becoming pervasive in modern society as seen in the proliferation of casinos, sports betting, lottery and bingo. Investing in the stock market does not fit the definition of gambling in the sense that stocks or other securities are purchased and are not lost but fluctuate in value. However, playing the stock market does fit

---

151 Keep your lives free from the love of money and be content with what you have, because God has said, "Never will I leave you; never will I forsake you."(Heb 13:5)

152 He who works his land will have abundant food, but he who chases fantasies lacks judgment. (Pr 12:11)

153 The sluggard's craving will be the death of him, because his hands refuse to work. All day long he craves for more, but the righteous give without sparing. (Pr 21:25-26)
For even when we were with you, we gave you this rule: "If a man will not work, he shall not eat." (2Th 3:10)

154 Then he said to them, "Watch out! Be on guard against all kinds of greed; a man's life does not consist in the abundance of his possessions." (Lk 12:15)

155 You shall not covet your neighbor's wife. You shall not set your desire on your neighbor's house or land, his manservant or maidservant, his ox or donkey, or anything that belongs to your neighbor." (Dt 5:21)

the idea of accumulating significant wealth without working. The retirement funds of many Americans depend on the rising value of the stock market. The best way to avoid the risk of divine judgment in this area is to invest only in securities that offer a guaranteed rate of return without risk to the principle. The accumulation of wealth through lending and charging a fair interest is approved by the Bible.[156]

---

156 You may charge a foreigner interest, but not a brother Israelite, so that the Lord your God may bless you in everything you put your hand to in the land you are entering to possess. (Dt 23:20)

Discussion Questions

1. Do you think gambling is a sin? List reasons that you agree or disagree.

2. Gambling is taxed in many states and becomes a significant source of revenue. Do you think this is a good thing? List reasons, pros and cons.

3. Promoters of gambling generally tout the creation of jobs and more traffic that benefits local businesses as positive economic impacts. What has your experience of this been?

4. What are some games played by children for fun that are like gambling?

5. I've heard people say that sports betting in fantasy pools or among friends is a harmless way to enhance the excitement of sporting events. What do you think of this?

6. Most compulsive gamblers began to gamble before they were fourteen. What are some warning signs that might indicate a child could develop a gambling problem?

7. Legalized gambling is one of the fastest growing markets in the United States. Gross revenue from all forms of gambling in the United States is greater than what Americans spend on movie tickets, theme parks, spectator sports and videogames combined![157] Do you think this reflects a change in priorities or values among Americans?

---

157 *PBS NineNet, Frontline, Gambling Facts & Stats,* http://www.pbs.org/ wgbh/pages/frontline/shows/gamble/etc/facts.html

Good Works

Popular human reasoning says that doing good works makes better people out of those who do them. An extension of this thinking is that, if enough good deeds can be done, then God will grant the doer great rewards, including eternal life with him in heaven. Those deeds that God judges to be good will be rewarded without partiality.[158] God will judge all the actions of each person and determine whether they are good or bad and God will reward or punish accordingly.[159]

Galatians 6:7 says that each person will reap what they sow although what the rewards will be is not specified because they are beyond human understanding or expression.[160] There is no clear evidence in the Bible that the rewards God gives for good deeds include eternal life. On the contrary, the Bible says that man is not

---

158   Since you call on a Father who judges each man's work impartially, live
      your lives as strangers here in reverent fear. (1Pe 1:17)

159   I will strike her children dead. Then all the churches will know that I am
      he who searches hearts and minds, and I will repay each of you according
      to your deeds. (Rev 2:23)
      "Behold, I am coming soon! My reward is with me, and I will give to
      everyone according to what he has done." (Rev 22:12)

160   However, as it is written: "No eye has seen, no ear has heard, no mind has
      conceived what God has prepared for those who love him." (1Co 2:9)

justified by doing good (i.e. keeping God's laws) but rather by faith in Jesus Christ.[161] Eternal life with God in heaven is a gift given by him to those who believe in Jesus Christ as savior. Therefore, it cannot be earned or bestowed by any human actions such as by baptism or other sacraments.[162] God has chosen some to be saved by grace, which is his unmerited favor.[163] Those who are saved are chosen not as a result of anything they have done but because of the mercy and purposes of God, which cannot be fully understood.[164]

The Bible teaches that all men are dead spiritually because of their sins.[165] It is by the work of the Holy Spirit that believers are transformed into children of God and heirs of heaven; not the result of human actions or will.[166]

161　know that a man is not justified by observing the law, but by faith in Jesus Christ. So we, too, have put our faith in Christ Jesus that we may be justified by faith in Christ and not by observing the law, because by observing the law no one will be justified. (Gal 2:16)

162　For it is by grace you have been saved, through faith—and this not from yourselves, it is the gift of God—not by works, so that no one can boast. (Eph 2:8-9)

163　So too, at the present time there is a remnant chosen by grace, and if by grace, then it were no longer by works; if it were, grace would no longer be grace. (Ro 11:5-6)

164　So do not be ashamed to testify about our Lord, or ashamed of me his prisoner. But join with me in suffering for the gospel, by the power of God, who has saved us and called us to a holy life—not because of anything we have done but because of his own purpose and grace. (2Ti 1:8-9)

165　As for you, you were dead in your transgressions and sins, in which you used to live when you followed the ways of this world and the ruler of the kingdom of the air, the spirit who is now at work in those who are disobedient. (Eph 2:1-2)

166　he saved us, not because of righteous things we had done, but because of his mercy. He saved us through the washing of rebirth and renewal by the Holy Spirit, whom he poured out on us generously through Jesus Christ our Savior, so that, having been justified by his grace, we might become heirs having the hope of eternal life. (Tit 3:5-7)

The desire to do good works as defined and directed by God comes from experiencing the presence of God inside of every born again believer. Therefore, good works are the expression, confirmation, and evidence of genuine saving faith or of being born again or born spiritually into the kingdom of God.[167] Saving faith is more than intellectual assent. It transforms thoughts and conduct, and is the result of the indwelling presence of the Holy Spirit.[168] Spiritual birth is followed by internal changes that transform believers according to God's will and plans, which result in visible good deeds.[169]

It is through good deeds that believers experience the presence and pleasure of God in increasing measure. Works done from a motivation to express love for God and obedience to his will revealed in the Bible, and prayer, build an ever-closer relationship. God chooses to interact most frequently and powerfully with those who seek and obey him.[170]

167　he saved us, not because of righteous things we had done, but because of his mercy. He saved us through the washing of rebirth and renewal by the Holy Spirit, whom he poured out on us generously through Jesus Christ our Savior, so that, having been justified by his grace, we might become heirs having the hope of eternal life. (Tit 3:5-7)

168　What good is it, my brothers, if a man claims to have faith but has no deeds? Can such faith save him? Suppose a brother or sister is without clothes and daily food. If one of you says to him, "Go, I wish you well; keep warm and well fed," but does nothing about his physical needs, what good is it? In the same way, faith by itself, if it is not accompanied by action, is dead. (Jas 2:14-17)

169　Don't you know that you yourselves are God's temple and that God's Spirit lives in you? If anyone destroys God's temple, God will destroy him; for God's temple is sacred, and you are that temple. (1Co 3:16-17)
　　 Do you not know that your body is a temple of the Holy Spirit who is in you, whom you have received from God? You are not your own; you were bought at a price. Therefore honor God with your body. (1Co 6:19-20)

170　Therefore, my dear friends, as you have already obeyed—not only in my presence, but now much more in my absence—continue to work out your salvation with fear and trembling, for it is God who works in you to will and to act according to his good purpose. (Php 2:12-13)

Every deed, whether good or evil, is known to God and each person will be judged by them.[171] Therefore, every moment of every day is significant regarding rewards and punishment in the next life. While salvation or being declared forgiven of sins depends on faith and not works, each person will receive differing rewards or punishments in heaven or hell. First Corinthians 3:13-15 says that believers will have their good works tested by fire. Those deeds done with motives based on pride, self-image, wealth, or anything other than the will of God will not count toward eternity. All believers will enter heaven based on their faith in Jesus as their savior. However, rewards will be based on obedience to Jesus as Lord and so some will have few rewards if they don't seek to obey his lordship on earth (i.e. they will pass through the fire of God's judgment but suffer loss).[172]

Unbelievers also will be judged according to their deeds, which may imply different levels of suffering in hell or possibly just that they had not received Jesus as savior and so their sins warrant eternal punishment in hell.[173]

---

171 And we know that in all things God works for the good of those who love him, who have been called according to his purpose. (Ro 8:28)

172 his work will be shown for what it is, because the Day will bring it to light. It will be revealed with fire, and the fire will test the quality of each man's work. If what he has built survives, he will receive his reward. If it is burned up, he will suffer loss; he himself will be saved, but only as one escaping through the flames. (1Co 3:13-15)

173 And I saw the dead, great and small, standing before the throne, and books were opened. Another book was opened, which is the book of life. The dead were judged according to what they had done as recorded in the books. The sea gave up the dead that were in it, and death and Hades gave up the dead that were in them, and each person was judged according to what he had done. Then death and Hades were thrown into the lake of fire. The lake of fire is the second death. If anyone's name was not found written in the book of life, he was thrown into the lake of fire. (Rev 20:12-15)

Discussion Questions

1. It is a common value taught to children from a young age that hard work merits rewards. Therefore, it is natural to believe that God owes us something for good works. What is wrong with this thinking?

2. How would you define good works? Name some examples of good works. How do these examples compare with what the Bible says?

3. What is the difference between doing good and good works that merit rewards by God?

4. Are good works related to our relationship with God? If so, do they help define who we are in the Body of Christ?

5. The Parable of the Workers in the Vineyard (Matthew 20) tells of a man (who in the traditional Christian understanding, represents God) who hires some workers early in the day, some later, and some an hour before quitting time, then pays each of them the same amount. In this story, work is rewarded not based on hourly effort but on the will of God. What does this story tell us about God and how he judges good works?

6. Do you think there is an expectation that people who are Christians from a young age and faithfully do good works will be rewarded more than someone who becomes a believer late in life? Does the parable of the Workers in the Vineyard change this view?

7. Do you think it is possible to do good works that are not pleasing to God and for which there will be no rewards?

8. What kind of rewards do you expect from God? List some rewards that are realized now and discuss ideas of what future rewards in heaven might be like. (Jn 14: 1-4).

9. Is it possible for those who are lost to do good works worthy of reward in God's view? If not, how do you explain the fact that lost people do good deeds?

10. What should be the motivation for doing good works? (Heb 12:2)

Heaven

The word heaven has several meanings in the Bible. Paul refers to the third heaven in 2 Corinthians 12:2, which he describes as paradise and a place of inexpressibly beautiful and wondrous things that he was not permitted to tell.[174] This third heaven is the highest of the heavens described in the Bible. The other two heavens mentioned are the sky and the stars.[175] This highest heaven is God's dwelling place from which he hears men's prayers and observes their actions.[176]

---

174 And I know that this man—whether in the body or apart from the body I do not know, but God knows—was caught up to paradise. He heard inexpressible things, things that man is not permitted to tell. (2Co 12:3-4)

175 But will God really dwell on earth? The heavens, even the highest heaven, cannot contain you. How much less this temple I have built! (1Ki 8:27)

176 Look down from heaven, your holy dwelling place, and bless your people Israel and the land you have given us as you promised on oath to our forefathers, a land flowing with milk and honey. (Dt 26:15)
Hear the supplication of your servant and of your people Israel when they pray toward this place. Hear from heaven, your dwelling place, and when you hear, forgive. (1Ki 8:30)

While God is omnipresent, heaven is a place where his presence is fully revealed.[177] God sits on a throne in heaven and his presence inspires joy, praise, and worship among those creatures that are deemed faithful and worthy to dwell with him.[178] Heaven is sometimes referred to as the Kingdom of God, where everything and everyone are in complete harmony with his will.[179] In contrast, hell is described as a place where those who are judged unworthy will be shut out from the presence of God.[180]

The throne of God is located in a temple in heaven.[181] The Ark of the Covenant is located in this temple.[182] Revelation 4 says that

---

177 Where can I go from your Spirit? Where can I flee from your presence? If I go up to the heavens, you are there; if I make my bed in the depths, you are there. (Ps 139:7-8)
   To him who is able to keep you from falling and to present you before his glorious presence without fault and with great joy—(Jude 24)

178 After this I looked and there before me was a great multitude that no one could count, from every nation, tribe, people and language, standing before the throne and in front of the Lamb. They were wearing white robes and were holding palm branches in their hands. And they cried out in a loud voice: "Salvation belongs to our God; who sits on the throne, and to the Lamb." All the angels were standing around the throne and around the elders and the four living creatures. They fell down on their faces before the throne and worshipped God," (Rev 7:9-11)
   All this is evidence that God's judgment is right, and you will be counted worthy of the kingdom of God, for which you are suffering. (2 Th 1:5)

179 "As the weeds are pulled up and burned in the fire, so it will be at the end of the age. The Son of Man will send out his angels, and they will weed out of his kingdom everything that causes sin and all who do evil. They will throw them into the fiery furnace, where there will be weeping and gnashing of teeth. Then the righteous will shine like the sun in the kingdom of their Father. He who has ears, let him hear. (Mt 13:40-43)

180 They will be punished with everlasting destruction and shut out from the presence of the Lord and from the majesty of his power. (2 Th 1:9)

181 The Lord is in his holy temple; the Lord is on his heavenly throne. He observes the sons of men; his eyes examine them. (Ps 11:4)

182 Then God's temple in heaven was opened, and within his temple was seen the ark of his covenant. And there came flashes of lightning, rumblings, peals of thunder, an earthquake, and a great hailstorm. (Rev 11:19)

surrounding the throne are other lesser thrones and a sea of what is described as glass clear as crystal. Twenty-four elders sit on the lesser thrones and worship God, along with creatures, angels, and saints. From the throne, the glory and power of God are manifested in flashes of lightening, peals of thunder, and brilliant, unapproachable light.[183] Satan has access to the throne of God as an accuser of men until he is cast out during the future final judgment of the earth.[184] Angels move between heaven and earth in the service of God.[185]

There is some evidence that suggests that the location of heaven is above the earth.[186] In Psalm 102:19, God looks down upon the earth from heaven. However, the idea of up and down could also

---

183 Out of the brightness of his presence bolts of lightning blazed forth. The Lord thundered from heaven; the voice of the Most High resounded. (2Sa 22:13-14)
From the throne came flashes of lightning, rumblings, and peals of thunder. Before the throne, seven lamps were blazing. These are the seven spirits of God. (Rev 4:5)

184 One day the angels came to present themselves before the Lord and Satan also came with them. (Job 1:6)
Then there was war in heaven. Michael and his angels fought against the dragon, and the dragon and his angels fought back. But he was not strong enough, and they lost their place in heaven. The great dragon was hurled down—that ancient serpent called the devil, or Satan, who leads the whole world astray. He was hurled to the earth and his angels with him. (Rev 12:7-9)

185 He had a dream in which he saw a stairway resting on the earth, with its top reaching to heaven, and the angels of God were ascending and descending on it. (Ge 28:12)
Suddenly a great company of the heavenly host appeared with the angel, praising God and saying, "Glory to God in the highest, and on earth peace to men on whom his favor rests." When the angels had left them and gone into heaven, the shepherds said to one another, "Let's go to Bethlehem and see this thing that has happened, which the Lord has told us about." (Lk 2:13-15)

186 Great is the Lord, and most worthy of praise, in the city of our God, his holy mountain. It is beautiful in its loftiness, the joy of the whole earth. Like the utmost heights of Zaphon is Mount Zion, the city of the Great King. (Note: Zaphon can refer to a sacred mountain or the direction north.) (Ps 48:1-2)

refer to greater and lesser rather than direction. Jesus looks up to heaven to pray to the Father before performing the miracle of the loaves and fishes.[187] Jesus also ascended up to heaven.[188]

Jesus said that there are many dwelling places in heaven and that he prepares one for each believer.[189] These dwellings appear to include the total transformation of believers into a glorious state like Jesus rather than just a location or position in heaven.[190] Believers will be rewarded in heaven for earthly actions that are pleasing to God.[191] These rewards can be accumulated and stored up in heaven.[192]

While heaven is a place beyond the sky and stars, it is also close, as can be seen during the baptism of Jesus.[193] In these verses, heaven is opened and God the Father spoke from heaven while the Holy Spirit descended upon Jesus. One explanation of how heaven can be both remote and near is that it has more dimensions than in our world. These dimensions can be collapsed or expanded by God. An

---

187 Taking the five loaves and the two fish and looking up to heaven, he gave thanks and broke them. Then he gave them to the disciples to set before the people. (Lk 9:16)

188 After the Lord Jesus had spoken to them, he was taken up into heaven and he sat at the right hand of God. (Mk 16:19)

189 In my Father's house are many rooms; if it were not so, I would have told you. I am going there to prepare a place for you. (Jn 14:2)

190 Now we know that if the earthly tent we live in is destroyed, we have a building from God, an eternal house in heaven, not built by human hands. (2Co 5:1-2)

191 For the Son of Man is going to come in his Father's glory with his angels, and then he will reward each person according to what he has done. (Mt 16:27)

192 Do not store up for yourselves treasures on earth, where moth and rust destroy, and where thieves break in and steal. But store up for yourselves treasures in heaven, where moth and rust do not destroy, and where thieves do not break in and steal. (Mt 6:19-20)

193 When all the people were being baptized, Jesus was baptized too. And as he was praying, heaven was opened and the Holy Spirit descended on him in bodily form like a dove. And a voice came from heaven: "You are my Son, whom I love; with you I am well pleased." (Lk 3:21-22)

excellent book on this subject is entitled *Beyond the Cosmos* by Dr. Hugh Ross.

As mentioned, the word heaven can also refer to the sky or atmosphere of the earth.[194] The floodgates of heaven were opened and rain fell from the sky in the story of Noah's ark.[195] The word heaven is used to describe the building of the Tower of Babel.[196] Some examples of the use of the word heaven or sky to describe the location of the stars are found in Genesis 1:14 and 15:5.

God will create a new heaven and earth following the end of this age.[197] The new heaven and earth will no longer be separated and God will dwell on the new earth with men.[198] There will be a new city called Jerusalem, where God and believers will dwell. There is no temple in this city for God is its temple and the glory of God gives it light.[199] Nothing impure will ever enter it but only those whose names are written in the Lamb's book of life.[200]

---

194   God called the expanse "sky." And there was evening, and there was morning—the second day. (Ge 1:8)

195   Now the springs of the deep and the floodgates of the heavens had been closed, and the rain had stopped falling from the sky. (Ge 8:2)

196   Then they said, "Come let us build ourselves a city, with a tower that reaches to the heavens, so that we may make a name for ourselves and not be scattered over the face of the whole earth." (Ge 11:4)

197   Then I saw a new heaven and a new earth, for the first heaven and the first earth had passed away, and there was no longer any sea. (Rev 21:1)

198   And I heard a loud voice from the throne saying, "Now the dwelling of God is with men, and he will live with them. They will be his people, and God himself will be with them and be their God. (Rev 21:3)

199   I did not see a temple in the city, because the Lord God Almighty and the Lamb are its temple. The city does not need the sun or the moon to shine on it, for the glory of God gives it light, and the Lamb is its lamp. (Rev 21:22-23)

200   Nothing impure will ever enter it, nor will anyone who does what is shameful or deceitful, but only those whose names are written in the Lamb's book of life. (Rev 21:27)

Discussion Questions

1. What are some popular ideas about heaven from movies and books? Do they compare with what the Bible says?

2. What do you think heaven will be like? List some ideas and then read Revelation 21:10-22:5.

3. Do you think saints in heaven right now are aware of what is happening on the earth? Are there any Bible verses that support your view?

4. Where is heaven? Are there any indications in the Bible?

5. What is in heaven? Use a concordance to find some Bible passages that describe the things and appearance of heaven.

6. Find Bible verses that describe what happens in heaven. Do you think there will be eternal rest or will there be work to do in heaven?

Hell (What and Where)

Hell is a place of torment that was created by God for those angels that joined in Lucifer's attempt to challenge God.[201] There are indications in the Bible that hell may be inside of the earth. Hell is said to be "in the depths of the pit".[202] Christ descended into the earth after his crucifixion to free those held captive who were awaiting their redemption by his blood.[203] In Revelation 9:1-3, the devil, who is the star fallen from heaven described in Isaiah 14:12, is given authority to release demons upon the earth from the shaft

---

201 And the devil, who deceived them, was thrown into the lake of burning sulfur, where the beast and the false prophet had been thrown. They will be tormented day and night for ever and ever. (Rev 20:10)
How far you have fallen from heaven, O morning star, son of the dawn! You have been cast down to the earth, you who once laid low the nations! You said in your heart, "I will ascend to heaven; I will raise my throne above the stars of God; I will sit enthroned on the mount of assembly, on the utmost heights of the sacred mountain. I will ascend above the tops of the clouds; I will make myself like the Most High." But you are brought down to the grave, to the depths of the pit. (Isa 14:12-15)

202 They will bring you down to the pit, and you will die a violent death in the heart of the seas. (Eze 28:8)

203 They will bring you down to the pit, and you will die a violent death in the heart of the seas. (Eze 28:8)

of the abyss or pit in which they had been confined. Philippians 2:9-11 says that all creatures in heaven, on the earth, and under the earth will bow at the name of Jesus. The reference to creatures being "under the earth" only makes sense if this is where the demons and people in hell reside.

The devil is referred to as the ruler of the kingdom of the air.[204] During the temptation of Jesus, the devil offers Jesus his realm in the kingdoms of the world if Jesus will worship him.[205] These verses with others such as Isaiah 14:12-15 suggest that the evil and his angels have been cast to the earth and are largely confined to it. Satan has lost his place in heaven and even his access to the throne of God will be taken away before the final judgment in which he will be confined to the lake of fire forever.[206]

Hell is a place of torment where those who are there will be subject to intense fire and pain that will never end.[207] Some of the angels that joined with Lucifer in his rebellion against God have

---

204 As for you, you were dead in your transgressions and sins, in which you used to live when you followed the ways of this world and the ruler of the kingdom of the air, the spirit who is now at work in those who are disobedient. (Eph 2:1-2)

205 Again, the devil took him to a very high mountain and showed him all the kingdoms of the world and their splendor. "All this I will give you," he said, "if you will bow down and worship me." (Mt 4:8-9)

206 And there was war in heaven, Michael and his angels fought against the dragon, and the dragon and his angels fought back. But he was not strong enough, and they lost their place in heaven. The great dragon was hurled down—that ancient serpent called the devil, or Satan, who leads the whole world astray. He was hurled to the earth, and his angels with him. (Rev 12:7-9)

207 And if your eye causes you to sin, pluck it out. It is better for you to enter the kingdom of God with one eye than to have two eyes and be thrown into hell, where "their worm does not die, and the fire is not quenched." (Mk 9:47-48)

been bound in dark prisons until they are judged and cast into the lake of fire.[208]

In addition to the demons, people who have not believed in Jesus as their personal savior will also be cast into hell.[209] These people will be cast "body and soul" into hell.[210] People in hell suffer eternally and will be loathsome in appearance.[211] Hell is distinguished from the lake of fire which is the final destiny of Satan, fallen angels and people who do not believe in Jesus as their personal savior.[212]

All men have sinned and thus are headed to hell unless they come to God in a way that is acceptable to God.[213] Jesus said, "I am **the Way**, the Truth, and the Life and nobody comes to the Father (God) except through me."[214] The Bible says the way that leads to destruction (hell) is broad and there are many that go that way.[215]

The way to God is to ask Jesus to forgive you of your sins and to believe that his death on the cross paid for the punishment you deserve for your sins. Thus, salvation is a gift that is bestowed by

---

208 For if God did not spare angels when they sinned, but sent them to hell, putting them into gloomy dungeons to be held for judgment; (2Pe 2:4)

209 He will punish those who do not know God and do not obey the gospel of our Lord Jesus. They will be punished with everlasting destruction and shut out from the presence of the Lord and from the majesty of his power. (2Th 1:8-10)

210 Do not be afraid of those who kill the body but cannot kill the soul. Rather, be afraid of the One who can destroy both soul and body in hell. (Mt 10:28)

211 "And they will go out and look upon the dead bodies of those who rebelled against me; their worm will not die, nor will their fire be quenched, and they will be loathsome to all mankind." (Isa 66:24)

212 If anyone's name was not found written in the book of life, he was thrown into the lake of fire. (Rev 20:15)

213 for all have sinned and fallen short of the glory of God, (Ro 3:23)

214 Jesus answered, "I am the way and the truth and the life. No one comes to the Father except through me" (Jn 14:6)

215 Enter through the narrow gate. For wide is the gate and broad is the road that leads to destruction, and many enter through it. (Mt 7:13)

God on those who sincerely cry out to him and believe in him as their savior. It does not result from any good or religious works or ceremonies.[216]

John 1:12 says that those who believe in Jesus and receive him as savior will become children of God. Death and destruction in hell are a breath away for those who have not been born into God's kingdom.

My prayer is that all who read this earnestly call upon Jesus for salvation and experience the most precious and wonderful experience in life: the presence of Jesus in your very mind, soul, and entire being. Freedom from guilt, removing fear of God's wrath and eternal damnation in hell and replacing it with an eternal peace and joy that is indescribable and wonderful!

---

216 For it is by grace you have been saved, through faith—and this not from yourselves, it is the gift of God—not by works, so that no one can boast. (Eph 2:8-9)

Discussion Questions

1. What do you think hell is like? Use a concordance to find Bible verses to check your thoughts.

2. Some people do not believe in hell because they say such a place of eternal torment is not compatible with a God of love. What do you think of this reasoning?

3. List some reasons why soul sleep, annihilation and universalism are not compatible with the concepts of hell taught in the Bible. Why is each of these ideas appealing versus what the Bible teaches?

4. Where is hell? (Ac 2:31; Mt 12:40; Eph 4:9)

5. Do you think that those in heaven are aware of those suffering in hell? If so, what could be some reasons why God would allow such awareness to those in heaven?

6. There are over 162 references in the New Testament alone which warn of hell. *More than 70 of these references were uttered by the Lord Jesus Christ!* What does this say about those who teach that hell does not exist?

7. Hell comes to us directly from Old English *hel*. In Old English, *hel* is a black and fiery place of eternal torment for the damned. The Old Norse *hel* is a very cold place. It contrasts sharply with Valhalla, the hall of slain heroes.[217] How did the Viking culture affect what they believed about heaven and hell? Do you see this in modern cultures and religions?

---

217 *Answers, World History,* Middle English *helle,* from Old English, http://www.answers.com/topic/hell

How the World Was Created

The Bible says that God created everything.[218] I find no support for evolution in the Bible. In fact, not only did God create everything, but it was created in an orderly fashion: first, physical/chemical elements of air, light, water, and earth as described in Genesis 1:3-10; then plant life (verse 11); animals (verse 20-21, 24); and man last (verse 26-27). Throughout the first chapter of Genesis, there is a repetitious statement that God created each type of creature "according to their kinds."[219] In fact, the Hebrew word for kind means to portion out, separate or differentiate. Therefore, God created different creatures that were distinct from each other (i.e. species) and could only propagate as separate species.

Although man is learning to "re-engineer" species through new genetic knowledge and techniques, there is no evidence that species

---

218 In the beginning God created the heavens and the earth. (Ge 1:1)

219 Then God said, "Let the land produce vegetation: seed-bearing plants and trees on the land that bear fruit with seed in it, according to their various kinds." And it was so. (Ge 1:11)

have intermingled or gradually changed to form new species through natural processes. The genetic barriers that God established when he created life have been validated through thousands of years of human history in observing and manipulating the propagation of existing species.

No matter how much man strives to understand the origins of the universe and life on this planet, I believe the details of exactly how God created it will remain unknown to us in this life. The Bible gives us enough details to show clearly that we are created beings and are here because of the design and purpose of a higher life form and not by some improbable acts of chance. While we will never know all the details, there are some intriguing clues in the Bible that may shed light on some of the possible events of the past.

First, I want to stress that the ideas that I am about to present are somewhat speculative and are not meant to be dogmatic. Other interpretations are possible. Scientific evidence supports the idea that the earth is very old, while some Bible scholars have stated that our planet is less than ten thousand years old based on genealogies.

The Bible is the story of man's fall and redemption as revealed by God. Therefore, its focus is on the interaction of God with man. We know that there are historical facts and stories that preceded the age of man described in the Bible, such as the creation of angels and God's relationship with them. In fact, what the Bible says about angels, such as the fall of Lucifer (i.e. the devil), the announcements of Gabriel regarding Christ, and the ministries of angels relate to the story of man. There is undoubtedly much we don't know about the past and ongoing stories of God and angels. Therefore, the Creation story recorded in Genesis should be read as part of a larger story of God interacting with his creation.

With this perspective, Genesis 1:1 says that God created the heavens and earth "in the beginning," which could mean at some point prior to the age of man. If read in this way, there was an old earth created by God and inhabited by dinosaurs. This old age came to an end with a catastrophe that wiped out all (or at least much) of life on the earth. The fall of Lucifer from heaven to the earth recorded in Ezekiel 28:11-18 and Isaiah 14:12 could have been a cause of this destruction. Many scientists believe that the age of the dinosaurs ended due to a large meteor colliding with the earth. Could this have been a physical manifestation of Lucifer's fall from heaven?

In this view, Genesis 1:2 describes the condition of the earth at the end of the first age of the earth. The earth was formless and empty and darkness was over the surface of the deep. This could describe an earth enveloped by dust clouds as a result of a meteor impact and/or the fall of Lucifer. In verses 3-5 God begins by restoring the day and night cycle of the earth. This could correspond to the settling out or removal of suspended soil and smoke from the atmosphere. In verse 4, God separates the waters of the air from those of the land which is consistent with the idea of removing excessive water vapor and/or steam from the atmosphere and condensing it back onto the earth. Verses 6-8 describe actions taken by God to restore the atmosphere to conditions able to support life. In verse 9, God separates water from dry land and in verse 10 God creates land vegetation. Verses 14-19 appear to describe the final restoration of the atmosphere to a condition that we are familiar with where the stars and moon are visible at night. Verses 20-27 describe the orderly creation of increasingly complex life forms throughout the earth culminating in the creation of man.

The idea of God creating and recreating the earth is supported by verses that speak of the fact that the present earth and its ways will be consumed by fire and God will create a new heaven and earth.[220] God has created the present world order and will create another world order in the future without sin and death. According to this view, we are living in Middle Earth between the age of creatures past as evidenced by the fossil record and the future earth in which God will dwell with those who have been redeemed by the blood of Jesus. This new earth will be a place where there will be no more death, imperfection, or suffering.[221]

---

220 But the day of the Lord will come like a thief. The heavens will disappear with a roar; the elements will be destroyed by fire, and the earth and everything in it will be laid bare. Since everything will be destroyed in this way, what kind of people ought you to be? You ought to live holy and godly lives as you look forward to the day of God and speed it coming. That day will bring about the destruction of the heavens by fire, and the elements will melt in the heat. But in keeping with his promise, we are looking forward to a new heaven and a new earth, the home of righteousness. (2Pe 3:10-13)

221 And I heard a loud voice from the throne saying, "Now the dwelling of God is with men, and he will live with them. They will be his people, and God himself will be with them and be their God. He will wipe away every tear from their eyes. There will be no more death or mourning or crying or pain, for the old order of things has passed away." (Rev 21:3-4)

Discussion Questions

1. Some Christians think that God used evolution to create the world as we know it. What are some problems with trying to incorporate evolution into the Bible's account of creation?

2. Let's assume evolution is the way humans developed and go back in time to when there were no humans (*Homo sapiens*) but only their precursor species (*Homo erectus*?). One day a genetic change occurs in one individual of one tribe of *Homo erectus* such that this individual becomes a human. This individual can no longer produce offspring with other members of this tribe (or other tribes) and so dies without children. In order for there to be offspring, we have to postulate that two such changes occur in the tribe or in close enough proximity so that they can meet. Therefore, we need two genetic changes of the same type to create a new species. But wait! This is still not good enough because we need to have two such changes in members of the opposite sex compounding the improbability of this happening! These improbable events have to be repeated countless times to account for the many species that supposedly evolved from one other. Discuss this topic.

3. Do you believe humans co-existed with dinosaurs? If so, the popular view among scientists today is that dinosaurs were more like birds than slow moving reptiles. If this is so, humans would be severely challenged to survive in a world populated by a multitude of such creatures as the fossil record suggests (think Jurassic Park). What do you think?

4. After over 120 years of extensive and painstaking geological exploration on every continent and ocean bottom, formations have been discovered containing countless fossils. There are museums filled with over 100 million fossils of 250,000 different species. However, there is not one instance where there is clear evidence for one species transitioning from another, which is a fundamental requirement to prove the *theory* of evolution.[222] Why does the theory of evolution continue to be taught as factual science despite its problems?

5. Those who advocate evolution point to micro-evolution, genetic changes resulting in new species among simple organisms such as viruses and bacteria, as a proof of the larger theory. That this change happens in simple organisms is not disputed; that it results in more complex organisms (for example bacteria changing into multi-cellular organisms) has not been observed and that would be the real proof. Given the short life of bacteria and viruses, if we equate this to generations of humans, there should be millions of equivalent years of change. However, there have been no observed new and more complex organisms found from the micro-evolutionary changes. Only different species of bacteria and viruses! Why do you think species changes are limited to simple organisms such as viruses and bacteria?

---

222 *All About The Journey, Evolution & The Fossil Record,* Luther D. Sutherland, *Darwin's Enigma: Fossils and Other Problems,* 4th edition, Master Books, 1988, 9 http://www.allaboutthejourney.org/evolution-and-the-fossil-record.htm

Is God Fair?

When a child dies of cancer, a home is destroyed by a tornado or one neighbor is laid off while another is promoted, I sometimes hear people say "It's not fair." Some people live long lives and are wealthy while others live short lives in poverty. Some are taller, more attractive, talented, stronger, etc. It doesn't seem fair when the son of a vice president of a company is hired and promoted before others who may be more competent. We have all experienced things in our lives that do not seem fair. It's true that life is not fair but does this mean God is not fair?

Before we can answer this question, it is necessary to understand what is meant by being fair. Webster's Dictionary defines fairness as being just or adhering to a standard of righteousness or law without reference to personal inclinations. This also includes the idea of being impartial, unbiased and objective in viewing or judging people or things. The human idea of fairness includes the idea of treating everyone the same. At the core of this idea is the concept that life would be better if everyone was treated equally.

This is certainly true (or should be) in the matter of laws and respect for others. However, each person's life and experiences are unique reflecting the time and place accorded to us by God. It is futile to try to redesign society (through social programs or redistributing wealth) or people (through genetic engineering) to somehow make everyone equal. God has created us as unique individuals and this means that there will be inequities of talent, intelligence, beauty and anything else that is either desirable or undesirable.

The Bible teaches that men have a nature that is rebellious towards God.[223] Thus, mankind does not seek after God and we tend to do what offends Him. The result is that mankind is judged guilty of sin and the consequences are physical and spiritual death. God shows no favoritism and there are no exceptions in his view of mankind's sinful state.[224]Therefore, God is eminently pure and just in his judgment of all men. However, God also loves mankind and has provided one way for reconciliation through faith in Jesus Christ.[225]

From God's perspective, mankind is sinful and worthy of judgment. Because of his great love for us, he chose a very personal and painful remedy to provide reconciliation. While we were alienated in sin, he sent his son to suffer the death penalty that

---

223 Those who live according to the sinful nature have their minds set on what that nature desires; but those who live in accordance with the Spirit have their minds set on what the Spirit desires. The mind of sinful man is death, but the mind controlled by the Spirit is life and peace; the sinful mind is hostile to God. It does not submit to God's law, nor can it do so. Those controlled by the sinful nature cannot please God. (Ro 8:5-8)

224 Anyone who does wrong will be repaid for his wrong, and there is no favoritism. (Col 3:25).

225 This righteousness from God comes through faith in Jesus Christ to all who believe. There is no difference, for all have sinned and fall short of the glory of God, and are justified freely by his grace through the redemption that came by Christ Jesus. (Ro 3:22-24).

mankind deserved.[226] Thus, not only is God just but he is also loving and merciful.

What then causes people to complain about the unfairness of life and to conclude that there cannot be a God of love? It is usually painful grief at some loss or hardship that drives people to feel that they have been treated unfairly. During such times, it is natural to feel that we have been given more misfortune than others. However, it is precisely at such times that we must look to God for comfort and seek his purpose and view. God promises that all things work for good to those who love him and are called according to his purposes.[227] I believe that the inequities of this life are meant to point us to a sovereign God who has created inequities to bless and challenge us to seek him and be dependent upon him.

Dear Lord Jesus, please help me not to have a "poor me" attitude when some misfortune happens; help me to seek your purpose in suffering. Help me to remember that I am a clay vessel being shaped by you.[228]

---

226   But God demonstrates his own love for us in this: While we were still sinners, Christ died for us. (Ro 5:8).

227   And we know that in all things God works for the good of those who love him, who have been called according to his purpose. (Ro 8:28).

228   But who are you, O man, to talk back to God? Shall what is formed say to him who formed it, "Why did you make me like this?" Does not the potter have the right to make out of the same lump of clay some pottery for noble purposes and some for common use? (Ro 9:20-21).

Discussion Questions

1. If you could fix any five problems in the world today, what would they be? List responses and discuss.

2. If you could change any five things about yourself, what would they be?

3. In the previous two questions, were your answers self-centered or God centered?

4. When you compare yourself with others, do you tend to pick others who have more or less of wealth or desirable traits than you? Why is this? What kinds of emotions do you feel from these comparisons?

5. From a human perspective only, what would a completely fair world look like? How does this compare with reality?

6. What do you think is the role of Satan and demons in causing misery and bad things in life?

7. When bad things happen in life, why don't people blame the world, the "flesh" or the devil?

Judgment

The Bible says that all men will be judged by Jesus Christ.[229] There will be two outcomes to this judgment: either eternal life in heaven or condemnation in hell. Judgment occurs in two parts. The first happens after death and involves the soul (or mind) and spirit.[230] Paul says that, for believers, to be absent from the body is to be present

---

229 Moreover, the Father judges no one, but has entrusted all judgment to the Son, that all may honor the Son just as they honor the Father. He who does not honor the Son does not honor the Father, who sent him. "I tell you the truth, whoever hears my word and believes him who sent me has eternal life and will not be condemned; he has crossed over from death to life. I tell you the truth, a time is coming and has now come when the dead will hear the voice of the Son of God and those who hear will live. For as the Father has life in himself, so he has granted the Son to have life in himself. And he has given him authority to judge because he is the Son of Man. Do not be amazed at this, for a time is coming when all who are in their graves will hear his voice and come out—those who have done good will rise to live, and those who have done evil will rise to be condemned. (Jn 5:22-29)

230 Just as man is destined to die once, and after that to face judgment. (Heb 9:27)

with Jesus.[231] The second and final judgment will occur when the bodies of all who have died are resurrected and joined to their mind and spirit in either heaven or hell.[232]

God sets the time for judgment of each person.[233] He will judge all men fairly and without favoritism.[234] When those who are condemned are judged, they will be humbled and God will be exalted. There will be no other idols or distractions from God. They will tremble with fear in the presence of God and the things that consumed their attention will become worthless.[235]

---

231 Therefore we are always confident and know that as long as we are at home in the body we are away from the Lord. We live by faith, not by sight. We are confident, I say, and would prefer to be away from the body and at home with the Lord. (2Co 5:6-8)

232 Then I saw a great white throne and him who was seated on it. Earth and sky fled from his presence, and there was no place for them. And I saw the dead, great and small, standing before the throne, and books were opened. Another book was opened, which is the book of life. The dead were judged according to what they had done as recorded in the books. The sea gave up the dead that were in it, and death and Hades gave up the dead that were in them, and each person was judged according to what he had done. Then death and Hades were thrown into the lake of fire. The lake of fire is the second death. If anyone's name was not found written in the book of life, he was thrown into the lake of fire. (Rev 20:11-15)

233 You say, "I choose the appointed time; it is I who judge uprightly." (Ps 75:2)

234 Anyone who does wrong will be repaid for his wrong, and there will be no favoritism. (Col 3:25)

235 The Lord Almighty has a day in store for all the proud and lofty, for all that is exalted (and they will be humbled), for all the cedars of Lebanon, tall and lofty, and all the oaks of Bashan, for all the towering mountains and all the high hills, for every lofty tower and every fortified wall, for every trading ship and every stately vessel. The arrogance of man will be brought low and the pride of men humbled; the Lord alone will be exalted in that day, and the idols will totally disappear. Men will flee to caves in the rocks and to holes in the ground from dread of the Lord and the splendor of his majesty, when he rises to shake the earth. In that day men will throw away to the rodents and bats their idols of silver and idols of gold, which they made to worship. They will flee to caverns in the rocks and to the overhanging crags from dread of the Lord and the splendor of his majesty when he rises to shake the earth. (Isa 2:12-21)

Jesus shed blood on the cross to establish a new covenant of grace and mercy for those whose sins are forgiven by accepting Jesus as their personal savior and Lord.[236] God has shown his great patience and mercy for the past two thousand years in offering forgiveness of sins through Jesus.[237] God is slow to anger but will not leave the guilty unpunished.[238] At the end of the present age (i.e. the time of mercy and grace offered through Jesus), mankind will be judged and divided into those who enter the kingdom of God (i.e. heaven) or those thrown into the fiery furnace (i.e. hell).[239] Every person will be judged and rewarded according to what was done during their life.[240] Every deed by each person will be brought up at the time of judgment and nothing will be hidden.[241] Every spoken word will be

---

236 This is my blood of the covenant, which is poured out for many for the forgiveness of sins. (Mt 26:28)
He himself bore our sins in his body on the tree, so that we might die to sins and live for righteousness; by his wounds you have been healed. (1Pe 2:24)

237 For God so loved the world that he gave his one and only Son, that whoever believes in him shall not perish but have eternal life. For God did not send his Son into the world to condemn the world, but to save the world through him. Whoever believes in him is not condemned, but whoever does not believe stands condemned already because he has not believed in the name of God's one and only Son. (Jn 3:16-18)

238 The Lord is slow to anger and great in power; the Lord will not leave the guilty unpunished. His way is in the whirlwind and the storm, and clouds are the dust of his feet. (Na 1:3)

239 The Lord is slow to anger and great in power; the Lord will not leave the guilty unpunished. His way is in the whirlwind and the storm, and clouds are the dust of his feet. (Na 1:3)

240 and that you, O Lord, are loving. Surely you will reward each person according to what he has done. (Ps 62:12)

241 For God will bring every deed into judgment, including every hidden thing, whether it is good or evil. (Ecc 12:14)
For we must all appear before the judgment seat of Christ, that each one may receive what is due him for the things done while in the body, whether good or bad. (2Co 5:10)

judged.[242] Even the thoughts and intentions of each person will be judged and no details of each person's life will escape judgment.[243]

During the judgment, it will become clear that each person has sinned and deserves condemnation.[244] However, Jesus is the judge and therefore has the power to forgive sins and thereby justify those who have placed their faith in him.[245] Those who have rejected Jesus will be punished with everlasting destruction.[246] Satan, rebellious

---

242 But I tell you that men will have to give account on the day of judgment for every careless word they have spoken. (Mt 12:36)

243 He answered, "The one who sowed the good seed is the Son of Man. The field is the world, and the good seed stands for the sons of the kingdom. The weeds are the sons of the evil one, and the enemy who sows them is the devil. The harvest is the end of the age, and the harvesters are angels. As the weeds are pulled up and burned in the fire, so it will be at the end of the age. The Son of Man will send out his angels, and they will weed out of his kingdom everything that causes sin and all who do evil. They will throw them into the fiery furnace, where there will be weeping and gnashing of teeth. Then the righteous will shine like the sun in the kingdom of their Father. He who has ears, let him hear." (Mt 13:37-43)

244 The Lord is slow to anger and great in power; the Lord will not leave the guilty unpunished. His way is in the whirlwind and the storm, and clouds are the dust of his feet. (Na 1:3)

245 and that you, O Lord, are loving. Surely you will reward each person according to what he has done. (Ps 62:12)
Behold, I am coming soon! My reward is with me, and I will give to everyone according to what he has done. (Rev 22:12)

246 He will punish those who do not know God and do not obey the gospel of our Lord Jesus. They will be punished with everlasting destruction and shut out from the presence of the Lord and from the majesty of his power. (2 Th 1:8-9)
By the same word the present heavens and earth are reserved for fire, being kept for the day of judgment and destruction of ungodly men. (2 Pe 3:7)

angels and unbelievers will be thrown into the lake of fire to be tormented forever.[247]

Although believers in Jesus will not be condemned, they will be judged and receive rewards based on the merits of their actions.[248] Believers are told not to judge others because those who judge the faults of others may be guilty of the same faults and so they would be condemning themselves.[249]

Believers who judge themselves (i.e. acknowledge and repent of sins), will not be judged by God.[250] This appears to refer to the idea that believers are to confess and forsake sin.[251] Believers who do not judge themselves, confess, and forsake their sins impair their relationship with God. This variability in closeness of relationship with Jesus may translate to varying rewards in heaven indicated by the reference to the many mansions in heaven in John 14:2.

---

247   For the word of God is living and active. Sharper than any double-edged sword, it penetrates even to dividing soul and spirit, joints and marrow; it judges the thoughts and attitudes of the heart. Nothing in all creation is hidden from God's sight. Everything is uncovered and laid bare before the eyes of him to whom we must give account. (Heb 4:12-13)

248   He will punish those who do not know God and do not obey the gospel of our Lord Jesus. They will be punished with everlasting destruction and shut out from the presence of the Lord and from the majesty of his power. (2Th 1:8-9)
By the same word the present heavens and earth are reserved for fire, being kept for the day of judgment and destruction of ungodly men. (2Pe 3:7)

249   You, therefore, have no excuse, you who pass judgment on someone else, for at whatever point you judge the other, you are condemning yourself, because you who pass judgment do the same things. Now we know that God's judgment against those who do such things is based on truth. So when you, a mere man, pass judgment on them and yet do the same things, do you think you will escape God's judgment? (Ro 2:1-3)

250   But if we judged ourselves, we would not come under judgment. (1Co 11:31)

251   If we confess our sins, he is faithful and just and will forgive us our sins and purify us from all unrighteousness. (1Jn 1:9)

Discussion Questions

1. In Revelation 20:11-15, the Bible says that everything we have ever done will be judged, so every moment of our lives has eternal significance related to rewards and punishment. How does this view differ from the way we live? Why is this?

2. Most people admit that they have done things that are wrong but believe that their good deeds will outweigh the bad on judgment day. What does this say about the concept of God and sin?

3. Some people refuse to believe in hell because they see it as being inconsistent with the idea that God is loving and merciful. How do you respond to this? Find verses that support the idea that God is loving and merciful. Are these verses inconsistent with God's holy and just characteristics?

4. Jesus taught that forgiveness is not an option if we want to be forgiven. How does this apply to believers? Are we not forgiven of our sins when we are born again?

5. Christians generally believe that there is a judgment that happens to the spirit of each person after death. Based on this judgment, the spirit will go to heaven or hell or purgatory until the final judgment when bodies will be resurrected and reunited with their spirits. Purgatory is a temporary place of purification for sins that are not considered serious enough to warrant abiding in hell. What evidence is there in the Bible for judgment following death? What about purgatory?

Killing versus Murder

Physical and spiritual deaths are the result of the sinful actions of men.[252] God has the right to take life since he is the creator of it.[253] God will judge every action that results in the shedding of blood by any man or animal.[254] The right of governments to kill to maintain social order is attributed to Genesis 9:6 by many Bible scholars.

There are many examples in the Old Testament where God demanded the death penalty for Israelites who broke the laws he established. Death was the penalty for any parent who offered their child as a sacrifice to an idol.[255] Aberrant sexual behavior such as

---

252 For the wages of sin is death, but the gift of God is eternal life in Christ Jesus our Lord. (Ro 6:23)

253 See now that I myself am he! There is no god besides me. I put to death and I bring to life, I have wounded and I will heal, and no one can deliver out of my hand. (Dt 32:39)

254 And for your lifeblood I will surely demand an accounting. I will demand an accounting from every animal. And from each man, too, I will demand an accounting for the life of his fellow man. (Ge 9:5)

255 If the people of the community close their eyes when that man gives one of his children to Molech and they fail to put him to death, I will set my face against that man and his family and will cut off from their people both him and all who follow him in prostituting themselves to Molech. (Lev 20:4)

bestiality also warranted the death penalty.[256] God threatened to destroy the Israelites for rebelling against him.[257] He also ordained religious sacrifices that required the killing of animals.[258] From these verses, we deduce that God views killing people and animals as proper when done as he prescribes as a penalty or outcome of sins. In such cases, the governing authorities are to do the killing according to rules of law. Killing that occurs during wars between governments are also included to the degree that it is impersonal between the combatants.

A distinction is made between killing and murder in that killing is without evil intent and planning.[259] The death penalty was not required among the Israelites for accidental killings. In these cases, the killer could flee to a designated city of refuge and plead his case to the elders.[260] If the person is determined to have killed accidentally,

---

256 If a woman approaches an animal to have sexual relations with it, kill both the woman and the animal. They must be put to death; their blood will be on their own heads. (Lev 20:16)

257 The Lord said to Moses, "How long will these people treat me with contempt? How long will they refuse to believe in me, in spite of all the miraculous signs I have performed among them? I will strike them down with a plague and destroy them, but I will make you into a nation greater and stronger than they. (Nu 14:11-12)

258 The animals you choose must be year-old males without defect, and you may take them from the sheep or the goats. Take care of them until the fourteenth day of the month, when all must slaughter them at twilight. (Ex 12:5-6)

259 This is the rule concerning the man who kills another and flees there to save his life—one who kills his neighbor unintentionally, without malice aforethought. (Dt 19:4)

260 But if without hostility someone suddenly shoves another or throws something at him unintentionally or, without seeing him, drops a stone on him that could kill him, and he dies, then since he was not his enemy and he did not intend to kill him, the assembly must judge between him and the avenger of blood according to these regulations. The assembly must protect the one accused of murder from the avenger of blood and send him back to the city of refuge to which he fled. He must stay there until the death of the high priest, who was anointed with the holy oil. (Nu 35:22-25)

that person was to remain within the city of refuge until the death of the high priest or risk death at the hands of the victim's relatives.[261] If the killer was caught and killed outside the city of refuge, the victim's relative or avenger of blood was not considered guilty of murder but rather an executioner of God's laws as the accidental killer had placed himself beyond the mercy extended by God.

Murder is forbidden by the Ten Commandments and was also mentioned by Jesus.[262] Murder is planned and motivated by evil desires and emotions. It was Cain's jealousy, anger and pride that drove him to murder Abel.[263] David plotted to murder Uriah so he

---

261   But if the accused ever goes outside the limits of the city of refuge to which he has fled and the avenger of blood finds him outside the city, the avenger of blood may kill the accused without being guilty of murder. The accused must stay in his city of refuge until the death of the high priest; only after the death of the high priest may he return to his own property. (Nu 35:26-28)

262   You shall not murder. (Ex 20:13)
"Which ones?" the man inquired. Jesus replied, "Do not murder, do not commit adultery, do not steal, do not give false testimony" (Mt 19:18)

263   In the course of time Cain brought some of the fruits of the soil as an offering to the Lord. But Abel brought fat portions from some of the firstborn of his flock. The Lord looked with favor on Abel and his offering, but on Cain and his offering he did not look with favor. So Cain was very angry, and his face was downcast. Then the Lord said to Cain, "Why are you angry? Why is your face downcast? If you do what is right will you not be accepted? But if you do not do what is right, sin is crouching at your door; it desires to have you, but you must master it." Now Cain said to his brother Abel, "Let's go out to the field." And while they were in the field, Cain attacked his brother Abel and killed him. (Ge 4:3-8)
Do not be like Cain, who belonged to the evil one and murdered his brother. And why did he murder him? Because his own actions were evil and his brother's were righteous. (1Jn 3:12)

could cover up his affair with his wife Bathsheba.[264] King Herod had all of the male babies less than two years old murdered in Bethlehem in an attempt to destroy Jesus, whom, he feared, would one day be king.[265] The chief priests and teachers of the law planned to murder Jesus in a way that would not offend the people.[266] Jesus clarified that, in God's eyes, a person is accountable for murderous thoughts stemming from anger regardless of whether these thoughts are put into action.[267] Anyone who hates someone will be judged by God as a murderer.[268]

---

264 In the morning David wrote a letter to Joab and sent it with Uriah. In it he wrote, "Put Uriah in the front line where the fighting is fiercest. Then withdraw from him so he will be struck down and die." (2Sa 11:14-15) When Uriah's wife heard that her husband was dead, she mourned for him. After the time of mourning was over, David had her brought to his house, and she became his wife and bore him a son. But the thing David had done displeased the Lord. (2Sa 11:26-27)

265 When Herod realized that he had been outwitted by the Magi, he was furious, and he gave orders to kill all the boys in Bethlehem and its vicinity who were two years old and under, in accordance with the time he had learned from the Magi. (Mt 2:16)

266 Now the Passover and the Feast of Unleavened Bread were only two days away, and the chief priests and the teachers of the law were looking for some sly way to arrest Jesus and kill him. (Mk 14:1)

267 You have heard that it was said to the people long ago, "Do not murder, and anyone who murders will be subject to judgment." But I tell you that anyone who is angry with his brother will be subject to judgment. Again, anyone who says to his brother, "Raca," is answerable to the Sanhedrin. But anyone who says, "You fool!" will be in danger of the fire of hell. (Mt 5:21-22)

268 Anyone who hates his brother is a murderer, and you know that no murderer has eternal life in him. (1Jn 3:15)

Discussion Questions

1. How would you classify each of the following based on what the Bible says about killing versus murder?
- Death of terrorist in Iraq by U.S. soldiers
- A doctor gives a terminal cancer patient a lethal injection at the request of the patient
- A woman ends the life of her fetus
- Execution of a convicted criminal by the government
- Death of a driver in auto accident caused by a drunk driver
- Two men get into a fight over a woman and one dies
- The death of Abel at the hands of Cain
- The death of Bathsheba's husband in battle
- One person kills another in a fit of anger without planning it.
- A king orders a subject to be executed because he is not shown proper respect.
- Ethnic cleansing

2. One of the Ten Commandments is "Thou shalt not kill" yet God commands the Israelites to kill the people living in the Promised Land so that they can take possession of it. How do you explain this apparent contradiction?

3. Are there circumstances where homicide can be justified? Is there any evidence in the Bible to support your answer?

Marriage and Divorce

Marriage is God's idea and is the union of a man and woman in an intimate relationship.[269] The purpose of marriage is to provide companionship.[270] God created Eve as a complementary being to help Adam take care of the Garden of Eden.[271] Eve was created from a part (i.e. rib) of Adam.[272] Therefore, Eve was formed from the body of Adam, and God presented her to him. Eve is the missing piece of Adam's flesh that God took and fashioned into a similar yet uniquely different type of being. Adam and Eve were naked and yet

---

269 So the man gave names to all the livestock, the birds of the air, and all the beasts of the field. But for Adam, no suitable helper was found. So the Lord God caused the man to fall into a deep sleep; and while he was sleeping, he took one of the man's ribs and closed up the place with flesh. Then the Lord God made a woman from the rib he had taken out of the man, and he brought her to the man. The man said, "This is now bone of my bones and flesh of my flesh; she shall be called woman for she was taken out of man." For this reason a man will leave his father and mother and be united to his wife, and they will become one flesh. (Ge 2:20-24)

270 The Lord God said, "It is not good for the man to be alone. I will make a helper suitable for him." (Ge 2:18)

271 The Lord God took the man and put him in the Garden of Eden to work it and take care of it. (Ge 2:15)

272 Then the Lord God made a woman from the rib he had taken out of the man, and he brought her to the man. (Ge 2:22)

were not ashamed.[273] This indicates that they knew each other totally and loved and accepted each other just as each was.

The union of a man and woman in marriage is to completely fulfill sexual desires and is to exclude all others.[274] Marriage requires that the husband and wife fulfill each other's sexual needs.[275] It results in the husband and wife giving to each other rights to their bodies, which produces a one-flesh relationship. The strength of marriage depends on the commitment of each partner to the other. Therefore, marriage requires loyalty. Desiring another person outside of marriage is forbidden by the Ten Commandments.[276] Jesus said that even the mental act of desiring another outside of marriage is adultery.[277]

The intimacy and strength of the marriage relationship is compared to Christ and the church.[278] Husbands are to give themselves totally to their wives as Christ gave himself for the church. Husbands are to love their wives as their own body. Wives

---

273 The man and his wife were both naked, and they felt no shame. (Ge 2:25)

274 Drink water from your own cistern, running water from your own well. Should your springs overflow in the streets, your streams of water in the public square? Let them be yours alone, never to be shared with strangers. May your fountain be blessed, and may you rejoice in the wife of your youth. A loving doe, a graceful deer—may her breasts satisfy you always, may you ever be captivated by her love. (Pr 5:15-19)

275 The husband should fulfill his marital duty to his wife, and likewise the wife to her husband. The wife's body does not belong to her alone but also to her husband. In the same way, the husband's body does not belong to him alone but also to his wife. (1Co 7:3-4)

276 You shall not commit adultery. (Dt 5:18)

277 But I tell you that anyone who looks at a woman lustfully has already committed adultery with her in his heart. (Mt 5:28)

278 Husbands, love your wives, just as Christ loved the church and gave himself up for her to make her holy, cleansing her by the washing with water through the word, and to present her to himself as a radiant church, without stain or wrinkle or any other blemish, but holy and blameless. In the same way, husbands ought to love their wives as their own bodies. He who loves his wife loves himself. (Eph 5:25-28)

are to submit to their husbands as to the Lord.[279] The comparison of the relationship of husband and wife to Christ and the church says that the marriage relationship is to surpass all others in terms of intensity of love, unity, servant-hood and intimacy among human relations. In marriage, God joins a man and a woman together in a relationship that is so close that, from God's view, the two persons have become one and yet remain as distinct individuals.[280] This is a mystery that cannot be fully understood or explained. It is similar to Christ and the church and perhaps to the Trinity as well.

The Bible says that marriage is for life.[281] However, if a spouse dies, the remaining spouse is free to remarry but believers are only to remarry other believers.[282] A husband and wife must not deprive each other of sexual relations except by mutual consent.[283] If one partner is unfaithful, such as adultery and desertion, the faithful partner is not obligated to continue the marriage relationship.[284] If a person breaks the marriage covenant for any other reason, that person is

---

279   Wives, submit to your husbands as to the Lord. For the husband is the head of the wife as Christ is the head of the church, his body, of which he is the Savior. Now as the church submits to Christ, so also wives should submit to their husbands in everything. (Eph 5:22-24)

280   For this reason a man will leave his father and mother and be united to his wife, and the two will become one flesh. So they are no longer two, but one. Therefore, what God has joined together, let man not separate. (Mk 10: 7-9)

281   To the married I give this command (not I, but the Lord): A wife must not separate from her husband. But if she does, she must remain unmarried or else be reconciled to her husband. And a husband must not divorce his wife. (1Co 7:10-11)

282   A woman is bound to her husband as long as he lives. But if her husband dies, she is free to marry anyone she wishes, but he must belong to the Lord. (1Co 7:39)

283   Do not deprive each other except by mutual consent and for a time, so that you may devote yourselves to prayer. (1Co 7:5)

284   But if the unbeliever leaves, let him do so. A believing man or woman is not bound in such circumstances; God has called us to live in peace. (1Co 7:15)

committing adultery if another marriage is consummated.[285] Jesus said that other reasons given by Moses were not God's will but were due to the selfishness and rebellious nature of men.[286] God hates divorce.[287]

Sexual intercourse is more than just a physical union. Marriage is the most intimate human union and has mental, emotional, and spiritual components that are manifested in the act of intercourse. It is a covenant with God who commands faithfulness in marriage, which is the most sacred of human relationships.[288]

---

285 Anyone who divorces his wife and marries another woman commits adultery against her. And if she divorces her husband and marries another man, she commits adultery. (Mk 10:11)

286 "Why then," they asked, "did Moses command that a man give his wife a certificate of divorce and send her away?" Jesus replied, "Moses permitted you to divorce your wives because your hearts were hard. But it was not this way from the beginning." (Mt 19:7-8)

287 "I hate divorce," says the Lord God of Israel (Mal 2:16a)

288 Another thing you do: You flood the Lord's altar with tears. You weep and wail because he no longer pays attention to your offerings or accepts them with pleasure from your hands. You ask, "Why?" It is because the Lord is acting as the witness between you and the wife of your youth, because you have broken faith with her, though she is your partner, the wife of your marriage covenant. (Mal 2:13-15)

Discussion Questions

1. What are some common reasons for divorce? How many of these are related to selfishness, pride, communication or emotional problems?

2. Two common pillars found in most successful marriages are agreement in faith and money. Do you agree with that statement? Would you add anything else to this?

3. Make a list of the things you like most about your spouse. Compare notes with your spouse. Then make a class list according to gender. Discuss similarities and differences.

4. How can we better prepare children and young adults to choose wisely when considering a mate?

5. Discuss the role of TV and the movies on marital stability.

6. Do you think that lifestyles that bring men and women together during business travel and military assignments present more opportunities for adultery?

7. What things have you learned about marriage that you did not consider much or at all when you got married?

8. More than half the couples in the U.S. cohabit before marriage. Those who cohabited before marriage reported more conflicts and felt less secure and more likely to leave the relationship.[289] What are some reasons for this?

---

289 *About.com Marriage, Cohabitation Facts & Statistics,* http://marriage.about.
      com/od/cohabitation/qt/cohabfacts.htm

Miracles

Miracles are events observed or experienced by humans that are beyond human understanding or abilities and are caused by the willful actions of good and evil spiritual beings.

The Bible records many miracles, starting in Genesis with the creation of the world and ending in Revelation with a display of satanic power by the Antichrist and beast as well as God's judgments that culminate in the destruction of the Earth and the creation of a new one. At least thirty-five miracles performed by Jesus are recorded in the four gospels. Miracles can only be performed by humans as empowered by God, the devil or angels. Therefore, miracles are distinct from magical tricks, which appear to show unexplained abilities, but are based on deception. The occurrence of miracles is sometimes predicted such as the virgin birth of Jesus in Isaiah 7:14, but can also be spontaneous, such as those caused by the shadow of Peter in Acts 5:15-16.

Miracles are signs of the presence of good or evil spiritual beings beyond human comprehension or control. Believers are warned not to believe every spirit but to test them to see if they are from God.[290] One way to determine if a miracle is from God is to see if it confirms that Jesus is the Christ, versus pointing to someone or something else.[291] Other tests are to see if the miracle glorifies God and is consistent with the teachings or predictions of the Bible. Because miracles are powerful manifestations beyond human comprehension or control, great care and caution must be exercised to determine if they are good or evil. This is made more difficult by the fact that the devil seeks to deceive and confuse humans.[292]

The large number of miracles in the Bible shows that supernatural beings are involved in the affairs of men. While miracles are not a commonly recognized part of human existence, they do happen in diverse times and places and may go largely unnoticed.

Some of the miracles recorded in the Bible and their purpose(s) are summarized below.

---

290 Dear friends, do not believe every spirit, but test the spirits to see whether they are from God, because many false prophets have gone out into the world. (1Jn 4:1)

291 This is how you can recognize the Spirit of God: Every spirit that acknowledges that Jesus Christ has come in the flesh is from God, but every spirit that does not acknowledge Jesus is not from God. This is the spirit of the antichrist, which you have heard is coming and even now is already in the world. (1Jn 4:2-3)

292 And he performed great and miraculous signs, even causing fire to come down from heaven to earth in full view of men. Because of the signs he was given power to do on behalf of the first beast, he deceived the inhabitants of the earth. He ordered them to set up an image in honor of the beast who was wounded by the sword and yet lived. (Rev 13:13-14)

Purpose	Miracle	Reference
1. Power of God	Water to blood	Exodus 7:17
	Calming of sea	Matthew 8:23-27
	Lazarus raised	John 11:1-45
2. Presence of God	Pillars of cloud and fire	Exodus 13:21-22
	Tongues of fire	Acts 2:3
3. Provision of God	Manna	Exodus 16:13-35
	Loaves and fishes	Matthew 14:15-21
4. Protection of God	Pillar of cloud	Exodus 14:10-20
	Furnace survival	Daniel 3:19-27
	Poison snake bite	Acts 28:3-6
5. Sign of God's Will	Fleece test	Judges 6:36-40
	Angelic announcement	Luke 2:8-14
6. Jesus is Messiah	Cast out demons	Matthew 8:16-17
	Calm storm	Mark 4:35-41
	Walk on water	John 6:17-21
	Dead raised	Matthew 27:51-53
7. Gospel Validated	Signs and wonders	Acts 14:3
8. Answer to prayer	Angelic appearance	Daniel 10:2-14
	Peter's prison escape	Acts 12:5-18
9. Thwart God's Plan	Staffs become snakes	Exodus 7:8-12
10. Anti-Christ is God	Signs and wonders	2Thessalonians 2:8-12
11. Deceive humans	Call fire from sky	Revelation 13:11-15
	Miraculous signs	Revelation 16:14

The ability to perform miracles is mentioned as a spiritual gift that some believers are given.[293] In Galatians 3:5, Paul says that miracles occur among believers as a result of faith, not works. Jesus did not do many miracles in his hometown because the people there knew him as a child and ordinary man who now claimed to be the Messiah. Therefore, they did not have faith in him.[294]

293   Now you are the body of Christ, and each one of you is a part of it. And in the church God has appointed first of all apostles, second prophets, third teachers, then workers of miracles, also those having gifts of healing, those able to help others, those with gifts of administration, and those speaking in different kinds of tongues. (1Co 12:27-28)

294   And they took offense at him. But Jesus said to them, "Only in his hometown and in his own house is a prophet without honor." And he did not do many miracles there because of their lack of faith. (Mt 13:57-58)

Discussion Questions

1. Have you ever experienced a miracle? If so, describe it and make a list of common themes, types (such as healings) and circumstances.

2. Do you think miracles are common or rare? Do you view miracles as something spectacular or more mundane? Review the definition in the first part of this chapter.

3. What do you think of weeping statues, crosses of light, crop circles and ghosts?

4. List some of the miracles recorded in the Bible. Do they compare with those discussed in the previous questions?

5. Do you believe that there is a correlation between the strength of faith and the observance of miracles?

6. Some claim miracles associated with the images of Jesus and Mary appearing in such places as the skillet burns of a tortilla, rust stains on a 40-foot-high soybean oil tank, and the bathroom floor of a Texas auto parts store. Why do you think people get excited about such images? What is the difference between observing a genuine miracle and an active imagination?

7. Could a lack of fervent, vibrant faith among believers in America today be a reason why miracles seem less common than in the early church?

Money, Wealth, and Tithing

The Bible says that money accumulated into wealth is a reward for those who work diligently.[295] Money is a resource that is neither good nor evil in itself. However, what is done with it and our attitude toward it reflect our relationship with God. Jesus said that it is impossible to serve both God and money.[296] In preceding verses of Matthew 6, Jesus says that what is treasured or valued most is what one's heart is set on. The word "heart" as used here is from a Greek word that means mind or thoughts. Therefore, Jesus is warning that our attitude about money is determined by whether it is viewed as something from God or from one's self.

In Deuteronomy 8:17, there is a warning against the attitude that, "My power and the strength of my hands have produced this wealth for me." This attitude forgets that it is God who gives and sustains life and the abilities that enable the successful accumulation and enjoyment of money. Jesus illustrated this point in the story of

---

295 Lazy hands make a man poor, but diligent hands bring wealth. (Pr 10:4)

296 No one can serve two masters. Either he will hate the one and love the other, or he will be devoted to the one and despise the other. You cannot serve both God and Money. (Mt 6:24)

the wealthy man who planned to live a life of leisure for many years, but God called him a fool because that night he died and his wealth was hoarded for himself with no thought for God.[297]

The expenditure of money shows what is valued and what our priorities are despite what we may otherwise say. The love of money is a root of all kinds of evil.[298] Notice the Bible does not say that money is evil, but that the love of it reflects a selfish heart, which seeks self-will, power, and gratification. Those who love money never have enough and tend to hoard it to their own harm.[299]

Each of us will have to give an account of our deeds, including the use of money.[300] Therefore, seek to honor God by making it a

---

297 And he told them this parable: "The ground of a certain rich man produced a good crop. He thought to himself, 'What shall I do? I have no place to store my crops.' "Then he said, 'This is what I'll do. I will tear down my barns and build bigger ones, and there I will store all my grain and my goods. And I'll say to myself, 'You have plenty of good things laid up for many years. Take life easy; eat, drink and be merry.'" But God said to him, "You fool! This very night your life will be demanded from you. Then who will get what you have prepared for yourself? "This is how it will be with anyone who stores up things for himself but is not rich toward God." (Lk 12:16-21)

298 For the love of money is a root of all kinds of evil. (1Ti 6:10)

299 Whoever loves money never has money enough; whoever loves wealth is never satisfied with his income. (Ecc 5:10)
I have seen a grievous evil under the sun: wealth hoarded to the harm of its owner. (Ecc 5:13)

300 Now listen you rich people, weep and wail because of the misery that is coming upon you. Your wealth has rotted, and moths have eaten your clothes. Your gold and silver are corroded. Their corrosion will testify against you and eat your flesh like fire. You have hoarded wealth in the last days. (Jas 5:1-3)
And I saw the dead, great and small, standing before the throne, and books were opened. Another book was opened, which is the book of life. The dead were judged according to what they had done as recorded in the books. (Rev 20:12)

priority to give to him and he will bless you.[301] Paul warns against becoming proud as a result of riches or to trust in wealth which is uncertain.[302] He further says rather to put hope in God and be rich in good deeds, being generous and willing to share.

In doing these things, rewards will be stored up in the next life, which is a certain foundation for eternity.[303] Honoring God with money by giving him the first and best part as an expression of love and gratitude is the basis of tithing. The first mention of tithing in the Bible is when Abraham gave the priest Melchizedek a tenth of the spoils of battle in gratitude for the blessing given him.[304] Jacob vows to give God a tithe or tenth of all he has if God will provide for him and bless him.[305] The Israelites were commanded by God to give a tithe or tenth of everything they had to him.[306] God considers

---

301 Honor the Lord with your wealth, with the first fruit of all your crops; then your barns will be filled to overflowing, and your vats will brim over with new wine. (Pr 3:9-10)

302 Command those who are rich in this present world not to be arrogant nor to put their hope in wealth, which is so uncertain, but to put their hope in God, who richly provides us with everything for our enjoyment. (1Ti 6:17)

303 Command them to do good, to be rich in good deeds, and to be generous and willing to share. In this way they will lay up treasure for themselves as a firm foundation for the coming age, so that they may take hold of the life that is truly life. (1Ti 6:18-19)

304 Then Melchizedek king of Salem brought out bread and wine. He was priest of God Most High, and he blessed Abram, saying, "Blessed be Abram by God Most High, Creator of heaven and earth. And blessed be God Most High, who delivered your enemies into your hand." Then Abram gave him a tenth of everything. (Ge 14:18-20)

305 Then Jacob made a vow saying, "If God will be with me and will watch over me on this journey I am taking and will give me food to eat and clothes to wear so that I return safely to my father's house, then the Lord will be my God and this stone that I have set up as a pillar will be God's house, and of all that you give me I will give you a tenth." (Ge 28:20-22)

306 A tithe of everything from the land, whether grain from the soil or fruit from the trees, belongs to the Lord; it is holy to the Lord. (Lev 27:30)

failure of the Israelites to tithe as stealing from him.[307] God also promised far greater blessings than the value of the tithe to the Israelites if they would tithe.[308]

The ordinance of tithing is not mentioned in the New Testament, but the motivation to give to God is the same (i.e. an expression of love and gratitude).[309] Believers are to give cheerfully after prayerful consideration and not reluctantly or under compulsion.[310] Jesus said that it is not how much you give but how much of yourself you give that pleases God. In Luke 21:1-4, Jesus says that a widow, who gave two copper coins, gave more in God's eyes than the greater amounts of money given by the rich. Jesus knew that the widow gave all she had to live on, compared to the offerings of the rich that were but a fraction of their wealth.

In light of these things, how much should a Christian give? The answer is as much as one can freely and cheerfully give! Giving is a barometer or indicator of one's love for God. Giving is not to be done to have a good relationship with God, rather it is an outcome of a relationship which seeks to honor and please him. Giving should be continually increasing as our relationship and experience of God increase!

---

307 A tithe of everything from the land, whether grain from the soil or fruit from the trees, belongs to the Lord; it is holy to the Lord. (Lev 27:30)

308 Bring the whole tithe into the storehouse, that there may be food in my house. "Test me in this," says the Lord Almighty, "and see if I will not throw open the floodgates of heaven and pour out so much blessing that you will not have room enough for it." I will prevent pests from devouring your crops, and the vines in your fields will not cast their fruit," says the Lord Almighty. "Then all the nations will call you blessed, for yours will be a delightful land," says the Lord Almighty. (Mal 3:10-12)

309 This service that you perform is not only supplying the needs of God's people but is also overflowing in many expressions of thanks to God. (2Co 9:12)

310 Each man should give what he has decided in his heart to give, not reluctantly or under compulsion, for God loves a cheerful giver. (2Co 9:7)

Giving to God is not to be viewed as tax or legal obligation. It is an expression of love and gratitude by steward who sees it as a wise investment of his Master's resources. I have found that giving to God in this manner results in growth in generosity towards God that eventually results in the tithe becoming a floor which I do not want to fall below rather than a ceiling.

Discussion Questions

1. How has your attitude about giving money to the church and other Christian charities changed over the years? Has your motivation changed?

2. Do you think there is a relationship between the rise of government spending on social welfare programs in the U.S. in the past 60 years and the decline of attendance and commitment to Christian churches?

3. "At least one out of five American Christians gives literally nothing to church, para-church, or nonreligious charities," according to several national studies reported in the book *Passing the Plate: Why American Christians Don't Give Away More Money* by Christian Smith and Michael Emerson.[311] The remaining Christians give, on average, about 3 percent of pretax household income as annual donations to all religious and charitable causes. Do you know what the average amount is in your church? What difference would it make to the ministries of your church if the average was 10%?

4. When you receive your paycheck, do you look at it as an entitlement for your work or a blessing from God? What are some reasons for thinking of it as money given to you through the grace of God? How does thinking about money this way change your attitude about giving to God?

---

311   *2010 Large Church Finances and Staffing Report, Leadership Network, Warren Bird, 9.* http://christianstandard.com/2011/05/is-the-church-in-a-recession/

5. How is the amount of money given to God a barometer of your relationship to God?

6. What are some of the reasons why only one-third to one-half of U.S. church members financially support their churches?

Repentance Is More than Being Sorry

Repent is a word that is rarely used today and so is not well understood. A popular view is that it means to feel sorrow or be sorry about something. In the Bible, to repent means to have a change in thinking and attitude resulting in changed behavior. Sorrow may accompany this change but is not necessary to accomplish it.

This is summarized in 2 Corinthians 7:9-10, where Paul contrasts worldly and Godly sorrow. Worldly sorrow involves feelings of regret or loss but does not result in changed thinking or behavior. This is illustrated by Esau's sorrow in selling his birthright to Jacob for something to eat. In this case, Esau repented of this decision but the result could not be undone even though he wept and pleaded.[312]

---

312 See that no one is sexually immoral, or is godless like Esau, who for a single meal sold his inheritance rights as the oldest son. Afterward, as you know, when he wanted to inherit this blessing, he was rejected. He could bring about no change of mind, though he sought the blessing with tears. (Heb 12:16-17)

Paul says that worldly sorrow leads to death because it does not include a change in attitude or behavior toward God. Godly sorrow brings about repentance which produces an eagerness to make amends, see justice done, and get things right with God and mankind.[313] In 1 Kings 8:46-51, Solomon prays for his people and asks God to forgive them if they admit their sin and turn to him with all their heart. If the people show repentance toward God, he will forgive them and uphold their cause.[314]

Repentance involves admitting offending God, rejecting the offensive actions, and God's accepting these changes in thinking and behavior. Therefore, when John preached repentance, he was calling for people to see themselves as sinners needing Jesus as their personal savior.[315] Biblical repentance results in a change in attitude and

---

313 Godly sorrow brings repentance that leads to salvation and leaves no regret, but worldly sorrow brings death. See what this godly sorrow has produced in you: what earnestness, what eagerness to clear yourselves, what indignation, what alarm, what longing, what concern, what readiness to see justice done. At every point you have proved yourselves to be innocent in this matter. So even though I wrote to you, it was not on account of the one who did the wrong or of the injured party, but rather that before God you could see for yourselves how devoted to us you are. (2Co 7:10-12)

314 When they sin against you—for there is no one who does not sin—and you become angry with them and give them over to the enemy, who takes them captive to his own land, far away or near; and if they have a change of heart in the land where they are held captive, and repent and plead with you in the land of their conquerors and say, "We have sinned, we have done wrong, we have acted wickedly"; and if they turn back to you with all their heart and soul in the land of their enemies who took them captive, and pray to you toward the land you gave their fathers, toward the city you have chosen and the temple I have built for your Name; then from heaven, your dwelling place, hear their prayer and their plea, and uphold their cause. And forgive your people, who have sinned against you; forgive all the offenses they have committed against you, and cause their conquerors to show them mercy. (1Ki 8:46-50)

315 "The time has come," he said. "The kingdom of God is near. Repent and believe the good news!" (Mk 1:15)

behavior, which is referred to as a new heart and spirit.[316] It includes the idea of rejecting evil and turning or returning to God.[317] Godly repentance sometimes results in a public display of grief and distress, such as the practice of wearing sack clothing and ashes.[318]

God is involved in bringing men to repentance. Second Timothy 2:25-26 says God grants men repentance, leading them to knowledge of the truth. God speaks to man's mind and spirit, revealing offenses or sins and reconciliation in the atoning death of Jesus.[319] It is God's kindness, tolerance, and patience that lead men to repentance.[320] This verse implies interplay between the revelation of God and man's response (acknowledgement of sinfulness and lost condition). God is patient in dealing with men, encouraging a knowledge of sin and need for repentance.[321]

---

316   Therefore, O house of Israel, I will judge you, each one according to his ways, declares the Sovereign Lord. Repent! Turn away from all your offenses; then sin will not be your downfall. Rid yourselves of all the offenses you have committed, and get a new heart and a new spirit. Why will you die, O house of Israel? For I take no pleasure in the death of anyone, declares the Sovereign Lord. Repent and live! (Ez 18:30-32)

317   Therefore say to the house of Israel, This is what the Sovereign Lord says: Repent! Turn from your idols and renounce all your detestable practices! (Eze 14:6)

318   Therefore I despise myself and repent in dust and ashes. (Job 42:6)
Woe to you, Korazin! Woe to you, Bethsaida! If the miracles that were performed in you had been performed in Tyre and Sidon, they would have repented long ago in sack cloth and ashes. (Mt 11:21)

319   All this is from God, who reconciled us to himself through Christ and gave us the ministry of reconciliation: that God was reconciling the world to himself in Christ, not counting men's sins against them. And he has committed to us the message of reconciliation. (2Co 5:18-19)

320   Or do you show contempt for the riches of his kindness, tolerance and patience, not realizing that God's kindness leads you toward repentance? (Ro 2:4)

321   The Lord is not slow in keeping his promise, as some understand slowness. He is patient with you, not wanting anyone to perish, but everyone to come to repentance. (2Pe 3:9)

Repentance is an essential part of the good news of the gospel message that tells mankind how to be reconciled to God.[322] In Luke 13:3 Jesus said, "I tell you no! Unless you repent you too will all perish." Paul preached repentance, turning to God by acceptance of Jesus as savior and a changed life as evidence of a true salvation experience.[323] There is great joy in heaven over each sinner who repents.[324]

A key aspect of repentance is God's compassion and acceptance.[325] From the human perspective, it sometimes appears that God changes his mind but this is due to our linear view of time. There are many examples of God's conditional blessings or judgments involving the Israelites depending on their obedience to his commands.[326] The word repent sometimes is used to describe God's response (change

---

322 He told them, "This is what is written: The Christ will suffer and rise from the dead on the third day, and repentance and forgiveness of sins will be preached in his name to all nations, beginning at Jerusalem. (Lk 24:46-47)

323 First to those in Damascus, then to those in Jerusalem and in all Judea, and to the gentiles also I preached that they should repent and turn to God and prove their repentance by their deeds. (Acts 26:20)

324 I tell you that in the same way there will be more rejoicing in heaven over one sinner who repents that over ninety-nine righteous persons who do not need to repent. (Lk 15:7)

325 But as soon as they were at rest, they again did what was evil in your sight. Then you abandoned them to the hand of their enemies so that they ruled over them. And when they cried out to you again, you heard from heaven, and in your compassion you delivered them time after time. (Ne 9:28)

326 See, I am setting before you today a blessing and a curse—the blessing if you obey the commands of the Lord your God that I am giving you today; the curse if you disobey the commands of the Lord your God and turn from the way that I command you today by following other gods, which you have not known. (Dt 11:26-28)

of mind) to the repentance or rebellious actions of the nations.[327] This change of mind observed by humans in one-dimensional time appears as though God's thinking and plans change in response to human events. However, God is changeless and knows how all the events of time will unfold even before they happen. God's plans and purposes were established before the creation of the world; therefore, from God's eternal perspective, his thinking and plans do not change. The Bible states that he will have compassion on those he chooses.[328]

---

327 If at any time I announce that a nation or kingdom is to be uprooted, torn down, and destroyed, and if that nation I warned repents of its evil, then I will relent and not inflict on it the disaster I had planned. And if at another time I announce that a nation or kingdom is to be built up and planted, and if it does evil in my sight and does not obey me, then I will reconsider the good I had intended to do for it. (Jer 18:7-10)

328 Therefore God has mercy on whom he wants to have mercy, and he hardens whom he wants to harden. (Ro 9:18)

Discussion Questions

1. As parents we tend to teach our children to say they are sorry when they do something wrong. Is this good enough? What else should be taught?

2. John the Baptist practiced baptism of repentance. What do you think motivated the Jews to be baptized by him?

3. Jesus said that he wished to be baptized to "fulfill all righteousness." Is the baptism of Jesus related to repentance in any way?

4. "Repentance is more than a change of mind or feeling sorry for one's sins. It is a radical and deliberate turning or returning to God that results in moral and ethical change and action."[329] What role does the Holy Spirit play in causing repentance? Without the Holy Spirit, can there be genuine repentance?

5. Which comes first, repentance or turning from sin? What is the difference?

---

329 *Kenneth Barker, ed. Zondervan NASB Study Bible, Grand Rapids: Zondervan, 1999. p.1372.*

Sabbath or Sunday Worship

God created the earth in six days as described in the first chapter of Genesis. On the seventh day, God rested from his creation works.[330] God established the seventh day as a holy day of rest. Creation was complete and nothing further needed to be done. The Bible doesn't mention the significance of this to man until the time of Moses, when God commanded the Israelites to observe the seventh day of each week as a Sabbath day of rest.[331]

---

330 Thus the heavens and the earth were completed in all their vast array. By the seventh day God had finished the work he had been doing; so on the seventh day he rested from all his work. And God blessed the seventh day and made it holy, because on it he rested from all the work of creating that he had done. (Ge 2:1-3)

331 He said to them, "This is what the Lord commanded: 'Tomorrow is to be a day of rest, a holy Sabbath to the Lord. So bake what you want to bake and boil what you want to boil. Save whatever is left and keep it until morning.'" (Ex 16:23)
Bear in mind that this is why on the sixth day he gives you bread for two days. Everyone is to stay where he is on the seventh day; no one is to go out. So the people rested on the seventh day. (Ex 16:29-30)

The observance of the Sabbath was a sign of the everlasting covenant God established with the Israelites.[332] This covenant was a conditional promise to bless the Israelites and make them a chosen people through whom God would be honored, worshipped, and praised. The condition to bring this about required them to obey his commands that included the Sabbath observances.

The observance of the Sabbath day of rest is one of the Ten Commandments.[333] This commandment was directed specifically to the Israelites.[334] The Sabbath day is to remind the Israelites of their deliverance from slavery in Egypt through God's provision.[335] It is also a sign that they were his chosen people through whom the redemption of mankind from the penalty of sin would be accomplished by Jesus Christ. The penalty was death for any Israelite who failed to keep the Sabbath day of rest.[336] An Israelite man found

---

332   The Israelites are to observe the Sabbath, celebrating it for the generations to come as a lasting covenant. It will be a sign between me and the Israelites forever, for in six days the Lord made the heavens and the earth, and on the seventh day he abstained from work and rested. (Ex 31:16-17)

333   Remember the Sabbath day by keeping it holy. Six days you shall labor and do all your work, but the seventh day is a Sabbath to the Lord your God. On it you shall not do any work, neither you, nor your son, or daughter, nor your manservant or maidservant, nor your animals, nor the alien within your gates.
For in six days the Lord made the heavens and the earth, the sea, and all that is in them, but he rested on the seventh day. Therefore the Lord blessed the Sabbath day and made it holy. (Ex 20:8-11)

334   Say to the Israelites, "You must observe my Sabbaths. This will be a sign between you and me for the generations to come, so you may know that I am the Lord, who makes you holy. (Ex 31:13)

335   Say to the Israelites, "You must observe my Sabbaths. This will be a sign between you and me for the generations to come, so you may know that I am the Lord, who makes you holy. (Ex 31:13)

336   Observe the Sabbath, because it is holy to you. Anyone who desecrates it must be put to death; whoever does any work on that day must be cut off from his people. (Ex 31:14)

gathering wood on the Sabbath day was stoned to death.[337] Even lighting a fire was prohibited.[338] The only work allowed was the preparation of food.[339]

The Sabbath day of rest also applied to special holy days that the Israelites were commanded to observe, such as the Day of Atonement or Yom Kippur.[340] Once in the Promised Land, the Israelites were commanded not to do any work every seventh year so that the land would have a Sabbath rest.[341] No reaping or harvesting crops was permitted, but only whatever could be gathered naturally. This practice taught the Israelites to have faith in God and also served to

---

337 While the Israelites were in the desert, a man was found gathering wood on the Sabbath day. Those who found him gathering wood brought him to Moses and Aaron and the whole assembly, and they kept him in custody, because it was not clear what should be done to him. Then the Lord said to Moses, "The man must die. The whole assembly must stone him outside the camp." So the assembly took him outside the camp and stoned him to death, as the Lord commanded Moses. (Nu 15:32-36)

338 Do not light a fire in any of your dwellings on the Sabbath day. (Ex 35:3)

339 On the first day hold a sacred assembly, and another one on the seventh day. Do no work at all on these days, except to prepare food for everyone to eat—that is all you may do. (Ex 12:16)

340 This is to be a lasting ordinance for you: On the tenth day of the seventh month you must deny yourselves and not do any work—whether native-born or alien living among you—because on this day atonement will be made for you, to cleanse you. Then, before the Lord, you will be clean from all your sins. It is a Sabbath of rest, and you must deny yourselves; it is a lasting ordinance. (Lev 16:29-31)

341 The Lord said to Moses on Mount Sinai, "Speak to the Israelites and say to them: When you enter the land I am going to give you, the land itself must observe a Sabbath to the Lord. For six years sow your fields, and for six years prune your crops. But in the seventh year the land is to have a Sabbath of rest, a Sabbath to the Lord. Do not sow your fields or prune your vineyards. Do not reap what grows of itself or harvest the grapes of your untended vines. The land is to have a year of rest. Whatever the land yields during the Sabbath year will be food for you—for yourself, your manservant and maidservant, and the hired worker and temporary resident who live among you, as well as for your livestock and the wild animals in your land. Whatever the land produces may be eaten. (Lev 25:1-7)

focus their attention on him as provider and sustainer. All debts were also to be forgiven every seventh or Sabbath year, which served to remind them of the subservient role of money and things in honoring and serving God.[342]

Each Sabbath, the Israelites were to offer fermented wine, flour mixed with oil, and a lamb in the morning and evening.[343] These offerings were to be burned in the sanctuary as a pleasing aroma to the Lord. These Sabbath day burnt offerings were in addition to the daily burnt offerings, which also were two lambs, fermented drink, and grain.

Jesus became a priest of a new covenant that continues to offer forgiveness of sins through his shed blood on the cross.[344] This is in contrast to the Levitical priesthood based on the Mosaic covenant that required the sacrifice of animals whose shed blood did not take away men's sins in God's view.[345] Jesus is an eternal priest of a better

---

342 When the neighboring peoples bring merchandise or grain to sell on the Sabbath, we will not buy from them on the Sabbath or on any holy day. Every seventh year we will forgo working the land and will cancel all debts. (Ne 10:31)

343 This is the regular burnt offering instituted at Mount Sinai as a pleasing aroma, an offering made to the Lord by fire. The accompanying drink offering is to be a quarter of a hin of fermented drink with each lamb. Pour out the drink offering to the Lord at the sanctuary. Prepare the second lamb at twilight, along with the same kind of grain offering and drink offering that you prepare in the morning. This is an offering made by fire, an aroma pleasing to the Lord. On the Sabbath day, make an offering of two lambs a year old without defect, together with its drink offering and a grain offering of two-tenths of an ephah of fine flour mixed with oil. This is the burnt offering for every Sabbath, in addition to the regular burnt offering and its drink offering. (Nu 28:6-10)

344 In him we have redemption through his blood, the forgiveness of sins, in accordance with the riches of God's grace. (Eph 1:7)

345 But those sacrifices are an annual reminder of sins, because it is impossible for the blood of bulls and goats to take away sins. (Heb 10:3-4)

relationship between God and man.[346] This change means that there is a difference in the application of the Mosaic laws for those who enter into the covenant of grace through Jesus Christ.[347]

One of these changes was the Sabbath observance. Jesus performed miracles on the Sabbath and defended his disciples who gathered grain to eat.[348] These actions violated the Mosaic covenant laws and became one of the reasons some Pharisees decided to kill Jesus.[349]

---

346   Now there have been many of those priests, since death prevented them from continuing in office; but because Jesus lives forever, he has a permanent priesthood. Therefore he is able to save completely those who come to God through him, because he always lives to intercede for them. (Heb 7:23-25)

347   Now there have been many of those priests, since death prevented them from continuing in office; but because Jesus lives forever, he has a permanent priesthood. Therefore he is able to save completely those who come to God through him, because he always lives to intercede for them. (Heb 7:23-25)

348   At that time Jesus went through the grain fields on the Sabbath. His disciples were hungry and began to pick some heads of grain and eat them. When the Pharisees saw this, they said to him, "Look! Your disciples are doing what is unlawful on the Sabbath." He answered, "Haven't you read what David did when he and his companions were hungry? He entered the house of God, and he and his companions ate the consecrated bread—which was not lawful for them to do, but only for the priests. Or haven't you read in the Law that on the Sabbath the priests in the temple desecrate the day and yet are innocent? I tell you that one greater than the temple is here. If you had known what these words mean, 'I desire mercy, not sacrifice,' you would not have condemned the innocent. For the Son of Man is Lord of the Sabbath." (Mt 12:1-13)

349   But the Pharisees went out and plotted how they might kill Jesus. (Mt 12:14)

Believers in Jesus are free from the observance of the Sabbath and other special holy days dictated by the Mosaic covenant.[350] In Paul's day, Jewish Christians attempted to impose their Mosaic religious observances on gentile Christians. Paul's response was to say that believers have freedom from religious observances and what is permissible regarding food and drink.[351] Believers have entered into a Sabbath rest relationship with God through the blood of Jesus and thus rest from the need to do religious works to be accepted by God.[352]

Why do Christians meet on Sunday? The disciples of Jesus habitually met on Sunday for worship and prayer.[353] Jesus rose from the dead on the first day of the week.[354] The apostles were assembled

---

350 But now that you know God—or rather are known by God—how is it that you are turning back to those weak and miserable principles? Do you wish to be enslaved by them all over again? You are observing special days and months and seasons and years! (Gal 4:9-10)
Therefore do not let anyone judge you by what you eat or drink, or with regard to a religious festival, a New Moon celebration or a Sabbath day. (Col 2:16)

351 Therefore do not let anyone judge you by what you eat or drink, or with regard to a religious festival, a New Moon celebration or a Sabbath day. (Col 2:16)

352 There remains, then, a Sabbath rest for the people of God; for anyone who enters God's rest also rests from his own work, just as God did from his. Let us, therefore, make every effort to enter that rest, so that no one will fall by following their example of disobedience. (Heb 4:9-11)

353 On the first day of the week we came together to break bread. Paul spoke to the people and, because he intended to leave the next day, kept on talking until midnight. (Acts 20:7)
On the first day of every week, each one of you should set aside a sum of money in keeping with his income, saving it up, so that when I come no collections will have to be made. (1Co 16:2)

354 Early on the first day of the week, while it was still dark, Mary Magdalene went to the tomb and saw that the stone had been removed from the entrance. (Jn 20:1)

on sequential Sundays in the story of doubting Thomas.[355] Believers are commanded not to forsake assembling together and so meet on Sundays.[356] Jesus said that he came to fulfill the Jewish laws and not to discard them. (Mt 5:17) Sunday observance by Christians meets the intent of the Commandments to gather regularly and worship God.

---

355 On the evening of that first day of the week, when the disciples were together, with the doors locked for fear of the Jews, Jesus came and stood among them and said, "Peace be with you!" (Jn 20:19)
A week later his disciples were in the house again, and Thomas was with them. Though the doors were locked, Jesus came and stood among them and said, "Peace be with you!" (Jn 20:26)

356 Let us not give up meeting together, as some are in the habit of doing, but let us encourage one another—and all the more as you see the Day approaching. (Heb 10:25)

Discussion Questions

1. Many people have unique church and family traditions associated with Sunday. What do you do on Sunday that you do not do the rest of the week?

2. Discuss some of the various types of worship services, beliefs and practices that you are aware of among Christian churches. What are some of the reasons for these differences? Are any of them in conflict with the Bible?

3. Some Christians have Saturday worship services. Is this wrong? If so, why? Is there any support for your views in the Bible? Why have Saturday versus Sunday worship?

4. What do you think about Christians who do not go to church but watch Sunday worship services on television?

5. Name the elements of Sunday worship practiced in your church. What is the purpose for each? Is there any reason these elements should be in a certain order?

6. The word "liturgy" comes from a Greek word meaning *work of the people*. In other words, worship is something you do, not something you watch. Do worship services that rely on a strict format tend to make worshippers spectators instead of participants?

7. How do you think the worship services at your church could be improved?

Saints—Who Are They?

There are different Greek and Hebrew words used in the Bible referring to those who are called saints. In the Old Testament, the term holy one is synonymous with the word saint and is used to refer to angels as well as humans.[357] In the New Testament; a Greek word, *hagios*, is consistently used. This word means sacred, pure, blameless, consecrated, or most holy one. This word primarily refers to humans who are born again and are declared by God to be righteous through belief in the sacrifice of Jesus on the cross. Paul refers to the love that the saints or believers have for each other and the glorious inheritance that awaits them in heaven.[358] In Philippians 4:21-22, Paul refers to believers as saints who send their greetings to believers in other cities.

---

357 In the visions I saw while lying in my bed, I looked, and there before me was a messenger, a holy one, coming down from heaven. (Da 4:13)

358 For this reason, ever since I heard about your faith in the Lord Jesus and your love for all the saints, I have not stopped giving thanks for you, remembering you in my prayers. (Eph 1:15-16)
I pray also that the eyes of your heart may be enlightened in order that you may know the hope to which he has called you, the riches of his glorious inheritance in the saints. (Eph 1:18)

Psalm 116:15 says, "Blessed in the sight of the Lord is the death of his saints." Clearly, this only makes sense in reference to humans not angels. The meaning is the death of self-will and selfishness, to live according to our Lord's will for us, is pleasing in his sight.[359] *Hagios* is also used to describe holy people raised back to life when Jesus died.[360] The imprisonment of born again believers by Saul and the intercession of the Holy Spirit in helping believers are other examples of the use of this Greek word for saint.[361]

There are many other examples of the word saint referring to humans who are alive, resurrected, and in heaven. Therefore, the term saint in the Bible can refer to any human, alive or dead, who has been forgiven of their sins and declared by God to be holy. I find no support in the Bible for the view that saints are special persons declared by the church as worthy of elevated status. All born again

---

359 I have been crucified with Christ and I no longer live, but Christ lives in me. The life I live in the body, I live by faith in the Son of God, who loved me and gave himself for me. (Gal 2:20)
Therefore, I urge you, brothers, in view of God's mercy, to offer your bodies as living sacrifices, holy and pleasing to God—this is your spiritual act of worship. Do not conform any longer to the pattern of this world, but be transformed by the renewing of your mind. Then you will be able to test and approve what God's will is—his good, pleasing and perfect will. (Ro 12:1-2)

360 The tombs broke open and the bodies of many holy people who had died were raised to life. (Mt 27:52)

361 And that is just what I did in Jerusalem. On the authority of the chief priests I put many of the saints in prison, and when they were put to death, I cast my vote against them. (Acts 26:10)
In the same way, the Spirit helps us in our weakness. We do not know what we ought to pray for, but the Spirit himself intercedes for us with groans that words cannot express. And he who searches our hearts knows the mind of the Spirit, because the Spirit intercedes for the saints in accordance with God's will. (Ro 8:26-27)

believers alive or dead are saints because they are children of God through faith in Jesus and not because of works.[362]

Some Christian religions encourage praying to various saints who, in turn, ask God to grant their requests. This is a form of belief based on human logic and influence peddling that is not found in the Bible. The Bible teaches that we are to pray to God alone to meet our needs.[363] Praying to idols, statues, angels, or saints is idolatry and is forbidden.[364] Idolatry is any action that puts someone or something in the place of God. Therefore, praying to saints instead of to God is a form of idolatry.

Saints will judge the world and angels.[365] Believers will have a role in the final judgment of angels and humans who are condemned to hell. Exactly what is this role is not explained in the Bible, but it

---

362 Yet to all who received him, to those who believed in his name, he gave the right to become children of God—children born not of natural descent, nor of human decision or a husband's will, but born of God. (Jn 1:12-13)

he saved us, not because of righteous things we had done, but because of his mercy. He saved us through the washing of rebirth and renewal by the Holy Spirit, whom he poured out on us generously through Jesus Christ our Savior (Tit 3:5-7)

363 Do not be anxious about anything, but in everything, by prayer and petition, with thanksgiving, present your requests to God. And the peace of God, which transcends all understanding, will guard your hearts and your minds in Christ Jesus. (Php 4:6-7)

For there is one God and one mediator between God and men, the man Christ Jesus, who gave himself as a ransom for all men—the testimony given in its proper time. (1Ti 2:5)

364 The acts of the sinful nature are obvious: sexual immorality, impurity, and debauchery; idolatry and witchcraft; hatred, discord, jealousy, fits of rage, selfish ambition, dissentions, factions, (Gal 5:19-20)

Dear children, keep yourselves from idols. (1Jn 5:21)

365 If any of you has a dispute with another, dare he take it before the ungodly for judgment instead of before the saints? Do you not know that the saints will judge the world? And if you are to judge the world, are you not competent to judge trivial cases? Do you not know that we will judge angels? How much more the things of this life! (1Co 6:1-3)

does say that Jesus is the primary judge.[366] Saints will be judged and rewarded by God on an individual basis according to good works they have done in this life.[367] Therefore, saints will occupy different positions of honor depending on their love for and obedience to God.[368] Saints will be with God and have resurrected bodies similar to Jesus.[369]

The term Christian is not necessarily synonymous with the term saint. In Acts 11:26 those who followed the teachings of Christ and His apostles in the city of Antioch were first called Christians. The Greek word used for Christian in this passage means follower of Christ.

As we have seen above, those who are born again are saints, which is different from those who call themselves Christians. There are many church-going people in Christian churches who have not been born again and declared to be righteous (saints) in the eyes of God. In John 3:3 Jesus said, "…no one can see the kingdom of God

---

366 He commanded us to preach to the people and to testify that he is the one whom God appointed as judge of the living and the dead. (Acts 10:42) to the church of the firstborn, whose names are written in heaven. You have come to God, the judge of all men, to the spirits of righteous men made perfect. (Heb 12:23)

367 his work will be shown for what it is, because the Day will bring it to light. It will be revealed with fire, and the fire will test the quality of each man's work. If what he has built survives, he will receive his reward. If it is burned up, he will suffer loss; he himself will be saved, but only as one escaping through the flames. (1Co 3:13-15)

368 In my Father's house are many rooms; if it were not so, I would have told you. I am going to prepare a place for you. (Jn 14:2)

369 For the Lord himself will come down from heaven, with a loud command, with the voice of the archangel and with the trumpet call of God, and the dead in Christ will rise first. After that, we who are still alive and are left will be caught up together with them in the clouds to meet the Lord in the air. And so we will be with the Lord forever. (1Th 4:16-17)
Dear friends, now we are children of God, and what we will be has not yet been made known. But we know that when he appears, we shall be like him, for we shall see him as he is. (1Jn 3:2)

unless he is born again." There is a difference between born again Christians and those who are religious and declare themselves to be Christians but are not born again. Those who are born again are declared by God to be sons of light and children of God. Those who call themselves Christians but are not born again are like those whom Jesus rejects in Matthew 7:21-23. These people claim to be followers of Jesus and even minister in his name but have not experienced spiritual rebirth.

Discussion Questions

1. Humans many times seek power and influence by developing relationships with those of higher income or social status. Why is this? How does this relate to praying to cannonized saints?

2. Is there clear evidence from the Bible that those in heaven (saints) and those in hell know what is happening on the earth? Is there any inferential (indirect or unclear) evidence?

3. Why would a person desire to develop a prayer relationship with Mary, St. Francis of Assisi, Mother Theresa or some other recognized saint rather than with Jesus?

4. Moses, as well as the priests and prophets, acted as intermediaries for the Israelites, representing them before God. How is this similar or different from the practice of praying to saints?

5. Do you think that there are similarities between adopting patron saints to bring good fortune and good luck charms?

6. There are over 5,000 saints in the Roman Catholic Church that are patrons for many occupations and concerns in life. There are lists of patron saints for each day of the year. One such web site is: http://saints.sqpn.com

Salvation or How Do I Get to Heaven?

The main theme of the Bible is the fall of mankind from fellowship with God and the restoration of the relationship on an individual basis through faith in Jesus Christ.

The first step is personal acknowledgement of having offended God in many ways and therefore of having a sin problem. Romans 3:23 says that there is no one righteous in God's view, for all have sinned. Psalm 53:1-3 and Ecclesiastes 7:20 say that everyone has turned away from God and have become corrupted by their sins. Jesus said that those who acknowledge they are sick are those who seek help. Jesus also said that God calls sinners to salvation, not those who view themselves as good, or better than average.[370]

The second step is to admit that no amount of good deeds will make God owe us anything. Therefore, no amount of good works

---

370 On hearing this, Jesus said, "It is not the healthy who need a doctor, but the sick. But go and learn what this means: I desire mercy, not sacrifice. For I have not come to call the righteous, but sinners." (Mt 9:12-13)

will make God give us eternal life in heaven as a result. The Bible says that nobody can obtain righteousness with God by doing good deeds and obeying the law.[371] The failure to always do what is right results in awareness of our sinfulness. Religious sacrifices and ceremonies do not take away sins but rather serve as reminders of our sinfulness and God's holiness.[372]

How then can a person be made righteous with God and so be able to be in his presence in heaven? It is by believing and receiving Jesus Christ as your personal sin bearer.[373] The purpose of Jesus' life was to live a sinless life and then pay our sin debt by dying on the cross. Jesus bore our sins in his body on the cross and believers were healed by his wounds.[374] Christ died for sins, once for all, the righteous for the unrighteous, to bring believers to God.[375]

Romans 6:23 says that the wages of sin is death but the gift of God is eternal life through Jesus Christ. Jesus experienced death for

---

371 Therefore no one will be declared righteous in his sight by observing the law; rather, through the law we become conscious of sin. (Ro 3:20)

372 The law is only a shadow of the good things that are coming—not the realities themselves. For this reason it can never, by the same sacrifices repeated endlessly year after year, make perfect those who draw near to worship. If it could, would they not have stopped being offered? For the worshippers would have been cleansed once for all, and would no longer have felt guilty for their sins. But those sacrifices are an annual reminder of sins, because it is impossible for the blood of bulls and goats to take away sins. (Heb 10:1-4)

373 Yet to all who received him, to those who believed in his name, he gave the right to become children of God—children born not of natural descent, nor of human decision or a husband's will, but born of God. (Jn 1:12-13)

374 He himself bore our sins in his body on the tree, so that we might die to sins and live for righteousness; by his wounds you have been healed. (1Pe 2:24)

375 For Christ died for sins once for all, the righteous for the unrighteous, to bring you to God. He was put to death in the body but made alive by the Spirit. (1Pe 3:18)

us so that we might experience life through faith in him.[376] Jesus said, "I am the Way, the Truth and the Life, nobody comes to the Father except through me."[377] Acts 4:12 says that there is no other name given to men by which they can be saved from the penalty of their sins. Jesus said that all men are born once in a physical sense but only those who are born a second time in a spiritual sense can enter the kingdom of God.[378] This spiritual birth is not the result of any works done by men (such as baptism) but rather is an action of the Holy Spirit in response to faith in Jesus Christ.[379]

The third step in the process of restoration is to pray to Jesus to save you from the penalty of your sins by believing in him as your savior and receiving him as Lord. John 1:12 says that all who believe in Jesus as their savior and receive him as Lord are given the right to be children of God. Children of God are not born by human effort or will, but spiritually through the action of the Holy Spirit. Those that experience this spiritual birth in Christ become new creations reconciled to God and freed from the penalty of their sins.[380]

---

376   For what I received I passed on to you as of first importance: that Christ died for our sins according to the scriptures, that he was buried, that he was raised on the third day according to the scriptures. (1Co 15:3-4)

377   Jesus answered, "I am the way, the truth, and the life. No one comes to the Father except through me." (Jn 14:6)

378   In reply Jesus declared, "I tell you the truth, no one can see the kingdom of God unless he is born again." (Jn 3:3)

379   He saved us, not because of righteous things we had done, but because of his mercy. He saved us through the washing of rebirth and renewal by the Holy Spirit. (Tit 3:5)

380   Therefore, if anyone is in Christ, he is a new creation; the old has gone, the new has come! All this is from God, who reconciled us to himself through Christ and gave us the ministry of reconciliation. (2Co 5:17-18)

It is by faith, and not works, that people are born again and can enter into the kingdom and presence of God.[381] Jesus said that whoever hears his words and believes in him shall not perish but have everlasting life.[382]

---

381   For it is by grace you have been saved, through faith—and this not from yourselves, it is the gift of God—not by works, so that no one can boast. (Eph 2:8-9)
For God so loved the world that he gave his one and only Son, that whoever believes in him shall not perish but have eternal life. (Jn 3:16)

382   I tell you the truth, whoever hears my word and believes him who sent me has eternal life and will not be condemned; he has crossed over from death to life. (Jn 5:24)
But these things are written that you may believe that Jesus is the Christ, the Son of God, and that by believing you may have life in his name. (Jn 20:31)

Discussion Questions

1. Why do some think that salvation requires good works?

2. If good works do not merit salvation, what good are they?

3. Do church good works (baptism and communion) help to merit salvation more than personal good works?

4. Is it a natural tendency to want to prove one's salvation by speaking in tongues and doing good works? Why?

5. What is the self-test in 2 Corinthians 13:5 that is the correct way to assess one's salvation?

6. I have heard some teach that obedience or submission to Jesus is the proof of one's salvation. What do you think?

7. Read Philippians 2:12-13. What do these verses say about the will of man in doing good works?

8. In Matthew 7:15-20, Jesus says that false teachers will be known by their fruit. What does this mean? Does this also apply to the "good works" done by those who are not born again? See Matthew 7:21-23.

9. The fact that an individual is baptized or associates with other Christians does not mean that he or she has accepted salvation. Do you agree or not? What are some Bible verses that support your view?

Sexual Perversion

Homosexual relationships are described in the Bible as indecent and perverted behavior.[383] Such desires are said to be shameful lusts that are unnatural. Leviticus 18:22 says for a man to lie with another man as with a woman is detestable to God. Such behavior is described as unnatural and a form of rebellion against the order and ways that God established. Those who persist in homosexual relationships are among the wicked people listed in the Bible who will not inherit the kingdom of God.[384] This is to say that those who practice, condone, and promote sinful behavior such as homosexuality are in a state of

---

383 Because of this, God gave them over to shameful lusts. Even their women exchanged natural relations for unnatural ones. In the same way the men also abandoned natural relations with women and were inflamed with lust for one another. Men committed indecent acts with other men, and received in themselves the due penalty for their perversion. (Ro 1:26-27)

384 Do you not know that the wicked will not inherit the kingdom of God? Do not be deceived: Neither the sexually immoral nor adulterers nor male prostitutes nor homosexual offenders nor thieves nor the greedy nor drunkards nor slanderers nor swindlers will inherit the kingdom of God. (1Co 6:9-10)

opposition to God that will result in eternal punishment unless there is a change of heart and behavior.[385]

The people of Sodom and Gomorrah are mentioned in the Bible as examples of societies where sexual perversion was common. God punished this behavior by destroying these towns with fire and brimstone.[386] The men of Sodom gathered as a group at Lot's house and wanted to have sex with two visiting men who were actually angels in human form.[387] Lot tried to persuade them to have sex with his virgin daughters instead, but they insisted on having sex with the

---

385 Although they know God's righteous decree that those who do such things deserve death, they not only continue to do these very things but also approve of those who practice them. (Ro 1:32)
In a similar way, Sodom and Gomorrah and the surrounding towns gave themselves up to sexual immorality and perversion. They serve as an example of those who suffer the punishment of eternal fire. (Jude 1:7)

386 He looked down toward Sodom and Gomorrah, toward all the land of the plain, and he saw dense smoke rising from the land, like smoke from a furnace. So when God destroyed the cities of the plain, he remembered Abraham, and he brought Lot out of the catastrophe that overthrew the cities where Lot had lived. (Ge 19:28-29)

387 The two angels arrived at Sodom in the evening, and Lot was sitting in the gateway of the city. When he saw them, he got up to meet them and bowed down with his face to the ground. "My lords," he said, "please turn aside to your servant's house. You can wash your feet and spend the night and then go on your way early in the morning." "No," they answered, "we will spend the night in the square." But he insisted so strongly that they did go with him and entered his house. He prepared a meal for them, baking bread without yeast, and they ate. Before they had gone to bed, all the men from every part of the city of Sodom—both young and old— surrounded the house. They called to Lot, "Where are the men who came to you tonight? Bring them out to us so that we can have sex with them." (Ge 19:1-5)

two male visitors in Lot's house.[388] God's response to this wicked behavior was to destroy the town.[389]

The Bible also forbids other unnatural sexual acts such as bestiality. God commanded the Israelites that anyone who engaged in sexual relations with an animal must be put to death.[390] Leviticus 18:23 says that it is perversion in God's view for a woman to have sex with an animal. Anyone who had sex with an animal was cursed by God.[391]

The nation of Israel was warned that God would punish them if they became cursed because they did not obey God's commands.[392] Some may say that these curses applied only to the nation of Israel and not to modern societies. I do not find any Bible verses subsequent to these that would support this view. Therefore, I must conclude that God views any homosexual or animal sex acts as detestable and

---

388 Look, I have two daughters who have never slept with a man. Let me bring them out to you, and you can do what you like with them. But don't do anything to these men, for they have come under the protection of my roof. "Get out of the way," they replied. And they said, "This fellow came here as an alien, and now he wants to play the judge!" We'll treat you worse than them." They kept bringing pressure on Lot and moved forward to break down the door. (Ge 19:8-9)

389 The two men said to Lot, "Do you have anyone else here—sons-in-law, sons or daughters, or anyone else in the city who belongs to you? Get them out of here, because we are going to destroy this place. The outcry to the Lord against its people is so great that he has sent us to destroy it. (Ge 19:12-13)

390 Anyone who has sexual relations with an animal must be put to death. (Ex 22:19)
     If a man has sexual relations with an animal, he must be put to death, and you must kill the animal. If a woman approaches an animal to have sexual relations with it, kill both the woman and the animal. They must be put to death; their blood will be on their own heads. (Lev 20:15-16)

391 Cursed is the man who has sexual relations with any animal. Then all the people shall say, "Amen!" (Dt 27:21)

392 All these curses will come upon you. They will pursue you and overtake you until you are destroyed, because you did not obey the Lord your God and observe the commands and decrees he gave you. (Dt 28:45)

rebellious perversions of the natural order that God established. Any nation or society that tolerates or encourages such sexual behavior is subject to the wrath of God. If this is not so, God owes Sodom and Gomorrah an apology.

Discussion Questions

1. Should Christians oppose homosexual marriages? How should church members treat homosexuals who attend weekly services?

2. Why do you think Americans are less tolerant of sexual relations between adults and children than homosexuals?

3. Do you think that the increase in divorce and blended families has increased the opportunities for sexual relations between adults and children?

4. What is the role of the movies and television in changing attitudes about homosexuality? Can you name some movies in which the main characters were homosexuals or cross dressers? Discuss how these characters were portrayed especially if they seem to be good. What about talk shows and advertisements that feature homosexuals as wise, wholesome and good individuals?

5. How is homosexuality an act of rebellion against God?

6. Do you think that homosexuals should be allowed to adopt children or be in positions of trust with children, such as teachers?

Spiritual Gifts

Spiritual gifts are mentioned only in the New Testament. They are special abilities given by the Holy Spirit to believers to enable them to perform works of service.[393] Spiritual gifts are signs of God's presence and work in and through believers. These manifestations of the Holy Spirit are for the common good.

The result of the proper use of spiritual gifts is the strengthening of the one exercising the gifts and those blessed by receiving them.[394] Each born again believer in Jesus Christ has been given one or more spiritual gifts as God sees fit.[395] Believers are told to desire spiritual gifts, especially the gift of prophecy.[396] The word prophecy is from a

---

393　There are different kinds of gifts, but the same Spirit. There are different kinds of service, but the same Lord. There are different kinds of working, but the same God works all of them in all men. Now to each one the manifestation of the Spirit is given for the common good. (1Co 12:4-7)

394　I long to see you that I may impart to you some spiritual gift to make you strong—that is, that you and I may be mutually encouraged by each other's faith. (Ro 1:11)

395　We all have different gifts, according to the grace given us. If a man's gift is prophesying let him use it in proportion to his faith. (Ro 12:4-6)

396　Follow the way of love and eagerly desire spiritual gifts, especially the gift of prophecy. (1Co 14:1)

Greek word that has two meanings: to foretell events, and to speak or teach the truths of God as revealed by the Holy Spirit. This gift is particularly valuable in building up fellow believers through strengthening their understanding, encouraging them to pursue after God and his ways, and comforting them in their secure relationship and destiny with Christ in heaven.[397]

Believers have various gifts given by God, and are to exercise the gifts bestowed by God in proportion to their faith. I believe this means that each believer has an obligation to discover and use the gifts God gives, for the benefit of other believers. The depth and strength of a particular gift are no excuse for not sharing it. What is essential is that the gift be exercised in proportion to what God has given to his honor and to share the experience of the Holy Spirit.

For example, some may say that they are reluctant to teach because they are not good speakers or do not have anything sophisticated to share. If God has revealed some spiritual truth, share it! To not do so is to hoard it like the wicked servant who buried the talent given him.[398] This parable teaches that God expects us to use the talents he has given so that they will be multiplied.

Believers are warned not to be ignorant about spiritual gifts.[399] Believers are unified by the indwelling presence of the Holy Spirit

---

397 For anyone who speaks in a tongue does not speak to men but to God. Indeed, no one understands him; he utters mysteries with his spirit. But everyone who prophesies speaks to men for their strengthening, encouragement, and comfort. (1Co 14:2-3)

398 Then the man who had received the one talent came. "Master," he said, "I knew that you are a hard man, harvesting where you have not sown and gathering where you have not scattered seed. So I was afraid and went out and hid your talent in the ground. See, here is what belongs to you." His master replied, "You wicked, lazy servant! So you knew that I harvest where I have not scattered seed? Well then, you should have put my money on deposit with the bankers, so that when I returned I would have received it back with interest." (Mt 25:24-27)

399 Now about spiritual gifts, brothers, I do not want you to be ignorant. (1Co 12:1)

and form a spiritual body.[400] Just as the human body is composed of many parts with different functions, so is the body of believers organized into local church bodies.[401] Believers are to discover their spiritual gifts and contribute to the well-being of other believers. Believers are interdependent and indispensable to the spiritual health of the church to such a great extent that Paul says that, when one part suffers (or is dysfunctional), every part suffers. Conversely, when one part is honored (or strengthened), other believers are blessed.[402] The denial or refusal to pursue the full expression of spiritual gifts given by God diminishes the presence of the Holy Spirit in those believers of the local church.[403]

Much controversy surrounds defining spiritual gifts, and I do not intend to enter into this debate. Suffice it to say that I believe any actions prompted by the Holy Spirit in the lives of believers that glorify God and help believers are spiritual gifts. A table that presents some of the spiritual gifts mentioned in the Bible is included at the end of the chapter.

The one in whom the gift is working will experience the joy and pleasure of the presence of God in a new or stronger way. The exercise of spiritual gifts results in strengthening and confirming God's presence and relationship, resulting in an increase in the fruit of the Spirit evident in the life of the believer.[404]

---

400   The body is a unit, though it is made up of many parts; and though all its parts are many, they form one body. So it is with Christ. For we were all baptized by one Spirit into one body—whether Jews or Greeks, slave or free—and we were all given the one Spirit to drink. (1Co 12:12-13)

401   Now you are the body of Christ, and each one of you is a part of it. (1Co 12:27)

402   If one part suffers, every part suffers with it; if one part is honored, every part rejoices with it. (1Co 12:26)

403   Do not put out the Spirit's fire; (1Th 5:19)

404   But the fruit of the Spirit is love, joy, peace, patience, kindness, goodness, faithfulness, gentleness, and self-control. (Gal 5:22)

Look for unexpected insights and blessings that were not anticipated. An example is that many times while teaching God's Word, he reveals new truths from the feedback of others that are attributed to what the teacher said, but that the teacher did not intend. There is a multiplying effect to the blessings of the truth shared beyond what the teacher planned or even knew.

The lives of those exposed to the exercised gifts will be blessed and there will be spiritual growth manifested in increased faith, wisdom, knowledge and love, transforming the character and lives of believers.

Gift	Description	Reference
1.Prophecy/ Teaching	Foretelling Events	1 Corinthians 12:10
2. Service	Good Works	Romans 12:7; Galatians 6:10
3. Exhortation	Encouraging Believers	Hebrews 10:25; Romans 12:8
4. Giving	Generous Sharing	2 Corinthians 8:1-7; Romans 12:8
5. Wisdom	Correct Application of Knowledge	2 Peter 3:15-16
6. Knowledge	Intellectual and Experimental	Ephesians 4:11-14
7. Faith	Belief in and Seek after God	Hebrews 11:6
8. Administration	Organizing and Promoting Order	Titus 1:5
9. Evangelism	Proclaiming the Gospel	Ephesians 4:11-14
10. Pastor	Leader of the Local Church	1 Peter 5:1-3
11. Hospitality	Being Friendly and Sharing	1 Peter 4:9
12. Prayer	Requests, Intercession, and Thanks	James 5:14-16
13. Helper	Willing to Serve and Assist Others	1 Corinthians 12:28
14. Healing	Supernatural Physical and Emotional	1 Corinthians 12:9

Discussion Questions

1. Do you know what your spiritual gifts are? If not, there are spiritual gifts surveys that can help you identify them. Refer to 1 Corinthians 12:1-14; Romans 12:6-8 & Ephesians 4:11 for listings of spiritual gifts.

2. Make a list on the board of all of the gifts possessed by those present. Refer to the table in this chapter. Are there any gifts missing from the group? Are there other members of your church who are not present and who might have these gifts?

3. Do you think that speaking in tongues is a gift only for the early church leaders in reaching people of diverse languages as described in Acts or also for the present church? Find Bible verses to support your view.

4. Why is it important for believers to know and exercise their gifts in the church? What happens when believers who do not have the proper gifts try to perform ministries for which they are not empowered by the Holy Spirit?

5. What is the purpose of spiritual gifts?

Subjection to Government

The Bible says that "everyone must submit himself to the governing authorities, for there is no authority except that which God established".[405] God established the concept of human authority from the time of Noah to make men accountable for their actions and so have a means of deterring evil and destructive behavior.[406]

Imagine what life would be like without police and fire services, not to mention the armed forces. The Bible says that man has a corrupt nature that is prone to selfish behavior.[407] Without a social structure and consequences, men could steal, cheat, lie and kill on an unprecedented scale. Life as we know it would not be possible without the order and security provided by governments. Therefore,

---

405 Everyone must submit himself to the governing authorities, for there is no authority except that which God has established. (Ro 13:1)

406 And for your lifeblood I will surely demand an accounting. I will demand an accounting from every animal. And from each man, too, I will demand an accounting for the life of his fellow man. Whoever sheds the blood of man, by man shall his blood be shed; for in the image of God has God made man. (Ge 9:5-6)

407 The heart is deceitful above all things and beyond cure. Who can understand it? (Jer 17:9)
For out of the heart come evil thoughts, murder, adultery, sexual immorality, theft, false testimony, slander. (Mt 15:19)

the institution of government is a good concept that promotes order and harmonious human relationships.

At this point, some may say that not all governments promote good. In fact, there have been some very evil governments, such as Nazi Germany. Also, even good governments sometimes promote evil, such as the abortion laws in America. What is a Christian to do in these cases? Ultimately, God will judge all men according to their deeds.[408] Those deeds that God says are good will result in rewards, while those that he says are evil will result in punishment. Therefore, since God is our judge, we should be governed above all else by what he has revealed in the Bible.

In Jesus' day, the Roman Empire promoted taxation without adequate representation. In Matthew 22:21 Jesus says to give to Caesar what is due him and to God what is due him. Although Jesus said this in the context of paying taxes, the principle is to render to government the respect, obedience and service it is due and to do the same regarding God. Since God is the highest authority, man is to obey human government wherever it does not conflict with obeying God. In areas where human governments have evil laws, his people

---

408   For God will bring every deed into judgment, including every hidden thing, whether it is good or evil. (Ecc 12:14)
For we must all appear before the judgment seat of Christ, that each one may receive what is due him for the things done while in the body, whether good or evil. (2Co 5:10)
And I saw the dead, great and small, standing before the throne, and books were opened. Another book was opened, which is the book of life. The dead were judged according to what they had done as recorded in the books. (Rev 20:12)

are to obey God.[409] It is better to suffer temporarily in this life for doing good as defined by God than to lose rewards or suffer eternally in the next life.

Christians are told to live orderly lives and, as much as it depends on us, to be at peace with everyone.[410] There is no support in the Bible for insurrections or rebellions against the ruling authorities, even when the rulers were wicked tyrants such as Pharaoh, Nebuchadnezzar, Herod, or Caesar. As mentioned previously, Christians are called to submit to their governments and live good, humble and peaceful lives.[411] Therefore, resistance to evil must be within the framework of the governing authorities. We are to be obedient to God and strive to be holy. This may require breaking man's laws to obey God's laws. An example of this is seen in Daniel's refusal to worship the statue of Nebuchadnezzar.[412] Thus, Christians should work peacefully

---

409　Now when you hear the sound of the horn, flute, zither, lyre, harp, pipes, and all kinds of music, if you are ready to fall down and worship the image I made, very good. But if you do not worship it, you will be thrown immediately into a blazing furnace. Then what god will be able to rescue you from my hand? Shadrach, Meshach and Abednego replied to the king, "O Nebuchadnezzar, we do not need to defend ourselves before you in this matter. If we are thrown into the blazing furnace, the God we serve is able to rescue us from your hand, O king. (Da 3:15-17) Having brought the apostles, they made them appear before the Sanhedrin to be questioned by the high priest. "We gave you strict orders not to teach in this name," he said. "Yet you have filled Jerusalem with your teaching and are determined to make us guilty of this man's blood." Peter and the other apostles replied: "We must obey God rather than men!" (Acts 5:27-29)

410　If it is possible, as far as it depends on you, live at peace with everyone. (Ro 12:18)

411　Remind the people to be subject to rulers and authorities, to be obedient, to be ready to do whatever is good, to slander no one, to be peaceable and considerate, and to show true humility toward all men. (Tit 3:1-2)

412　But there are some Jews whom you have set over the affairs of the province of Babylon—Shadrach, Meshach and Abednego—who pay no attention to you, O king. They neither serve your gods nor worship the image of gold you have set up. (Da 3:12)

within the governing system to change laws opposed to Biblical teachings.

There are cases in the Bible where God uses one government to overthrow or conquer another, such as the Assyrian conquest of Israel due to the failure of the Israelites to obey God's commands.[413] Killing is justified in cases of civil justice, military conflict, or self-defense.[414] These cases have to do with interpersonal relationships or one governing authority versus another. Such cases do not rise to the level of the explicit directions given by Paul in Romans 13 regarding citizens of each government being subject to the authorities that God has ordained.

I have been raised to be proud of my American heritage as it relates to our forefathers rising up against a tyrannical king. However, I see no support for this in the Bible. At best, a case might be made that a new government was formed by the Continental Congress after the start of hostilities against England. I believe that God's way

---

413 The king of Assyria invaded the entire land, marched against Samaria and laid siege to it for three years. In the ninth year of Hoshea, the king of Assyria captured Samaria and deported the Israelites to Assyria. He settled them in Halah, in Gozan on the Habor River, and in the towns of the Medes. All this took place because the Israelites had sinned against the Lord their God, who had brought them up out of Egypt from under the power of Pharaoh, king of Egypt. They worshipped other gods and followed the practices of the nations the Lord had driven out before them, as well as the practices that the kings of Israel had introduced. (2Ki 17:5-8)

414 The Gadites and Rubenites said to Moses, "We your servants will do as our lord commands. Our children and wives, our flocks and herds will remain here in the cities of Gilead. But your servants, every man armed for battle, will cross over to fight before the Lord, just as our lord says." (Nu 32:25-27)
If anyone with malice aforethought shoves another or throws something at him intentionally so that he dies or if in hostility he hits him with his fist so that he dies, that person shall be put to death; he is a murderer. The avenger of blood shall put the murderer to death when he meets him. (Nu 35:20-21)
Be strong and let us fight bravely for our people and the cities of our God. The Lord will do what is good in his sight. (2Sa 10:12)

would have been for England to grant American independence, as he moves men's hearts.[415] This happened in England when the slave trade was abolished. Could America have been prematurely born, out of the impatience and shortsightedness of men?

---

415   and said: "O Lord, God of our fathers, are you not the God who is in heaven? You rule over all the kingdoms of the nations. Power and might are in your hand, and no one can withstand you.(2Ch 20:6)

Discussion Questions

1. Do you think it is right that tax dollars of Christians are used to provide abortion counseling and services? What should Christians do about this?

2. Should Christians ever advocate not obeying the laws of their country?

3. What does the Bible teach about slavery? What happened to the slave Philemon who had run away from his master to seek asylum with Paul?

4. Why is it important for Christians to be involved in their government?

5. What are some good organizations that advocate Christian values in government?

6. What do you think of the removal of the Ten Commandments and nativity scenes from public buildings? What is the role of religion in politics?

7. The President takes the oath of office on a Bible and Congress opens its business with prayer. The dollar bill says "In God We Trust." What should separation of church and state mean?

Swearing

There are several different types of expressions called swearing mentioned in the Bible.

Clearly, using God's name in any disrespectful way is forbidden.[416] Leviticus 19:12 says not to swear falsely by God's name and thereby profane the name of God. This means to use God's name in any manner that is irreverent (does not acknowledge the holiness and supremacy of God). God's name is certainly debased and used wrong in cursing and in common speech where his name is used to express anger. God's name is powerful and those who use it invoke the power of God for their own selfish purposes. It is interesting to note that even people who do not go to church and live immoral life styles invoke God's name regularly.

Examples of evil lifestyles are mentioned in Galatians 5:19-21 and include sexual immorality, witchcraft, hatred, jealousy, drunkenness, and participating in orgies. Those who practice such evil lifestyles, even if they do not believe in God, acknowledge his sovereignty and power by abusing his name. If there was no power

---

416   You shall not misuse the name of the Lord your God, for the Lord will not hold anyone guiltless who misuses his name. (Dt 5:11)

or meaning to God's name, why use it to express emotion or to emphasize a point in one's speech?

Another type of swearing was commanded by God to the Israelites.[417] In these cases, God says that the Israelites are only to swear oaths in his name and not that of anyone else. God would not tell his people to do this unless there was a proper way; otherwise there is a contradiction with the above verses prohibiting swearing. The key to resolving this apparent contradiction is to look at the context of these passages.

In both of the verses in Deuteronomy there is a command to fear God and to serve him exclusively. Therefore, this type of swearing may have been like a vow taken and sealed with God's name. It was a practice that was given to Israel for a period of time and has been rescinded by further revelation in the New Testament.

In Matthew 5:33-34, Jesus refers to this practice and then says that henceforth no swearing is allowed at all. "Do not swear at all: either by heaven, for it is God's throne, or by the earth, for it is his footstool; or by Jerusalem for it is the city of the Great King...Simply let your yes be yes and no, no, for anything beyond this comes from the evil one."

This command is repeated in James 5:12. We are not even to swear by ourselves since we do not have the power to make even one hair of our head turn black or white.[418] Therefore, all swearing that invokes the power and authority beyond what has been given to us is sin. We are not to take an oath or swear to bring something to pass since we have no power to guarantee it. Our lives are given

---

417 Fear the Lord your God, serve him only and take your oaths in his name. (Dt 6:13)
Fear the Lord your God and serve him. Hold fast to him and take your oaths in his name. (Dt 10:20)

418 And do not swear by your head, for you cannot make even one hair white or black. (Mt 5:36)

to us and we can die at any moment. How can we promise to bring about anything if life is not granted to us by God? Thus, to swear is to show disrespect to God, for in so doing man acts as though he has the power he does not possess. All future events are given to us by the will of God and so even common expressions such as "see you next week" should be phrased, "God willing, I will see you next week."

There is only one form of swearing that is not sinful. An example of this is when witnesses are sworn in a courtroom and an oath is taken to "Tell the truth, the whole truth and nothing else, so help me God." In this context, man is asking God to respectfully help in doing what is right and true. This invocation of power and authority is a plea, not a command, and acknowledges man's dependence on God.

Discussion Questions

1. Is the phrase "O my God!" a form of swearing?

2. What do you think of the word "awesome" used to describe something that is wonderful or good? Is this a form of swearing?

3. Is there anything wrong with the use of swear words to show strong emotion when something goes wrong?

4. Why is swearing offensive to God?

5. Why do you think God allowed the Israelites to swear by his name?

6. Are vows such as the Presidential oath of office or marriage vows a form of swearing?

7. How does putting thoughts into words make them more powerful? How does using God's name, hell or other spiritual words make thoughts powerful?

8. Is cursing without using God's name OK? What about using God's name to bless others such as "God bless you." Is this a form of swearing?

9. Swear words generally are related to God or to the body or bodily functions. Why is this?

10. Some people use swearing as a source of attention. Why?

The Church— Who and What Is It?

The Greek word for church (*ekklesia*) is found only in the New Testament, and means those who are called out, an assembly, congregation, or community of members on earth and/or in heaven. The church consists of believers in Jesus Christ, who are called to be saints.[419] As discussed in the chapter on saints, these are people who are born again and are thereby declared to be righteous in God's sight through the sacrifice of Jesus on the cross.[420] Therefore, the universal church consists of all born again believers, living and dead. On earth, believers associate into groups or congregations called

---

419 And you also are among those who are called to belong to Jesus Christ. To all in Rome who are loved by God and called to be saints. (Ro 1:6-7)

420 Everyone who believes that Jesus is the Christ is born of God, and everyone who loves the father loves his child as well. (1Jn 5:1)
For Christ died for sins once for all, the righteous for the unrighteous, to bring you to God. He was put to death in the body but made alive by the Spirit. (1Pe 3:18)

churches, which are further organized into sects or denominations of similar beliefs.

The Bible says that the church is the household of God and is the pillar and foundation of the truth.[421] Those who know Jesus as their personal savior know the truth necessary for eternal life.[422] This is the basis of the saving faith that is the good news of the gospel.[423]

The church is also called the family of believers.[424] There is a spiritual bond in the presence of the indwelling Holy Spirit that transcends denominations, relating all born again believers as children of God.

The church is also referred to as the body of Christ.[425] Just as a man and woman become one flesh through marriage, so Christ and the church (all born again believers) become one in spirit and likeness through Christ's redemption on the cross and the work of

---

421 Although I hope to come to you soon, I am writing you these instructions so that, if I am delayed, you will know how people ought to conduct themselves in God's household, which is the church of the living God, the pillar and foundation of the truth. (1Ti 3:14-15)

422 Jesus answered, "I am the way and the truth and the life. No one comes to the Father except through me." (Jn 14:6)
Yet to all who received him, to those who believed in his name, he gave the right to become children of God—children born not of natural descent, nor of human decision or a husband's will, but born of God. (Jn 1:12-13)

423 By this gospel you are saved, if you hold firmly to the word I preached to you. Otherwise you have believed in vain. For what I received I passed on to you as of first importance: that Christ died for our sins according to the scriptures, that he was buried, that he was raised on the third day according to the scriptures. (1Co 15:2-4)

424 Therefore, as we have opportunity, let us do good to all people, especially to those who belong to the family of believers. (Gal 6:10)

425 For the husband is the head of the wife as Christ is the head of the church, his body, of which he is the Savior. (Eph 5:23)

the Holy Spirit.[426] Each member of the church has a unique function, just as the different parts of the human body function for the good of the whole.[427] Just as the head coordinates and directs the parts of the physical body, so Jesus is the head of all believers and directs them as part of his spiritual body.[428]

The church consists of God's people, fellow citizens, and members of his household.[429] The foundation or basis for membership is faith in the revelation of God through the prophets and apostles regarding Jesus Christ as the savior of mankind.[430] Believers are intermingled with unregenerate religious people throughout local churches and denominations. No denomination- through religious

---

426 Husbands, love your wives, just as Christ loved the church and gave himself up for her to make her holy, cleansing her by the washing with water through the word, and to present her to himself as a radiant church, without stain or wrinkle or any other blemish, but holy and blameless. In this same way, husbands ought to love their wives as their own bodies. He who loves his wife loves himself. After all, no one ever hated his own body, but he feeds and cares for it, just as Christ does the church—for we are members of his body. "For this reason a man will leave his father and mother and be united to his wife, and the two will become one flesh." This is a profound mystery—but I am talking about Christ and the church. (Eph 5:25-32)
For those God foreknew he also predestined to be conformed to the likeness of his Son, that he might be the first born among many brothers. (Ro 8:29)

427 Now you are the body of Christ, and each one of you is a part of it. (1Co 12:27)

428 And God placed all things under his feet and appointed him to be head over everything for the church, which is his body, the fullness of him who fills everything in every way. (Eph 1:22-23)
And he is the head of the body, the church; he is the beginning and the firstborn from among the dead, so that in everything he might have the supremacy. (Col 1:18)

429 Consequently, you are no longer foreigners and aliens, but fellow citizens with God's people and members of God's household. (Eph 2:19)

430 For it is by grace you have been saved, through faith—and this not from yourselves, it is the gift of God—not by works, so that no one can boast. (Eph 2:8-9)

rituals, sacrifices, or sacraments- can guarantee the salvation of its members since spiritual birth is an action of the Holy Spirit in response to personal acceptance of Jesus Christ as savior by faith.[431]

In Matthew 16:18, there is a play on words in that Jesus says to Peter that he is a rock (*petros* or small stone in Greek) and on this rock (*petra* or massive rock referring to Jesus) is upon which the church will be built. Also, 1 Peter 2:4-8 speaks of Christ as the cornerstone, capstone, and stumbling stone, while believers are living stones built into a spiritual house. The statements by Jesus in Matthew 16:18-19 regarding Peter are in response to Peter's profession that Jesus is the Christ in Matthew 16:15-16. During the same conversation between Jesus and Peter in Matthew 16:23, Jesus calls Peter "Satan" and a stumbling block in response to Peter's statement in verse 22 that Jesus should not suffer and die.

I believe the keys to the kingdom of heaven referenced in Matthew 16:19 are the power and authority that was given not only to Peter but to all the apostles. This is supported by the fact that, in Matthew 18:18, Jesus repeats what he said to Peter but this time addresses all of the apostles.

Peter himself never claimed any special status among believers other than as an apostle by gift and an elder by office.[432] Three years after his conversion, Paul visited Peter and James in Jerusalem, presumably for instruction about Jesus and the gospel.[433] After

---

431   he saved us, not because of righteous things we have done, but because of his mercy. He saved us through the washing of rebirth and renewal by the Holy Spirit. (Tit 3:5)
     I tell you the truth, whoever hears my word and believes him who sent me has eternal life and will not be condemned; he has crossed over from death to life. (Jn 5:24)

432   Peter, an apostle of Jesus Christ, to God's elect, strangers in the world, scattered throughout Pontus, Galatia, Cappadocia, Asia, and Bithynia. (1Pe 1:1)

433   Then after three years, I went up to Jerusalem to get acquainted with Peter and stayed with him fifteen days. I saw none of the other apostles—only James, the Lord's brother. (Gal 1:18-19)

another fourteen years of preaching the gospel, primarily to the gentiles, Paul again goes to Jerusalem to meet with the leaders of the early church.[434] Paul mentions James, Peter, and John as leaders. In fact, the order of listing suggests that James, not Peter, was the prominent leader.

Later, when Paul and Peter were together in Antioch, Paul rebuked Peter for withdrawing from eating with gentile Christians.[435] Paul pointed out to Peter that he was not acting in line with the truth of the gospel.[436] From these verses, it is evident that Peter was not infallible in matters of religious doctrine and that he was not held in an elevated position above all other early Christian leaders.

I find no conclusive evidence in the Bible to support the idea that any one denomination is the "true" or "best" church. There are no perfect churches because there are no perfect groups of humans. The best churches are those that hold to the inerrancy and importance of the Bible, preach the gospel of salvation by faith in Jesus Christ, and encourage their members to seek a born again relationship with God through personal study of the Bible, prayer, and fellowship with other believers.

---

434   James, Peter, and John, those reputed to be pillars, gave me and Barnabas the right hand of fellowship when they recognized the grace given to me. They agreed that we should go to the gentiles, and they to the Jews. (Gal 2:9)

435   When Peter came to Antioch, I opposed him to his face, because he was clearly in the wrong. Before certain men came from James, he used to eat with the gentiles. But when they arrived, he began to draw back and separate himself from the gentiles because he was afraid of those who belonged to the circumcision group. The other Jews joined him in his hypocrisy, so that by their hypocrisy even Barnabas was led astray. (Gal 2:11-13)

436   When I saw that they were not acting in line with the truth of the gospel, I said to Peter in front of them all, "You are a Jew, yet you live like a gentile and not like a Jew. How is it, then, that you force gentiles to follow Jewish customs?" (Gal 2:14-16)

Discussion Questions

1. Say the word "church" and then list the words that come to mind. Group the words. Discuss these groups. Are there some that are more prevalent than others? Why is this? How do time, place, and culture affect the concept of "church?"

2. Have you ever been drawn to other believers that are different from you except for the presence of the Holy Spirit? Describe how your feelings towards these people would tend to be different without the bond of the Holy Spirit?

3. Read Matthew 18:18. What do you think Jesus meant? Do you think this power to forgive sins was a special authority granted to the apostles? How can this be since the meaning must be consistent with many Bible verses that say that sins are forgiven solely by faith in Jesus and that this is the work of the Holy Spirit and not of men (Eph 2:8-9; Titus 3:5; John 3:16-17).

4. There are over 1,500 Christian denominations in America today with diverse and sometimes conflicting beliefs. Why do you think there are so many Christian denominations? What are the strengths and weaknesses of such diversity?

The Feminine Side of God

Is there a feminine aspect to God? Most references to God in the Bible generally use masculine terms such as Father. However, Genesis 1:27 says "So God created man in his own image, in the image of God he created him; *male and female* he created them." What does this mean? First of all, we must attempt to remove the idea of human sexuality from the terms masculine and feminine as they might apply to God. Jesus said that there are no sexual relations after death but that people will be like the angels.[437] Although Jesus is masculine in his humanity, we must realize that God is described as a consuming fire and a spirit being.[438] Thus, God is more complex than our concepts of masculine and feminine. Also, the Bible clearly teaches that God is Triune or three persons in one being (see the Trinity Chapter). There is no credible support to suggest that there is a female being that is God.

---

437 Jesus replied, "You are in error because you do not know the Scriptures or the power of God. At the resurrection, people will neither marry nor be given in marriage; they will be like the angels in heaven." (Mt 22:29)

438 "God is spirit, and his worshippers must worship in spirit and in truth." (Jn 4:24)
For our God is a consuming fire. (Heb 12:29)

I believe that there are qualities and roles shown by God in the Bible that can be best described as feminine. The Greek word for wisdom frequently used in the Bible is *sophia*. This term is used to describe the wisdom that comes from God and has feminine connotations. It is by the power of the Holy Spirit that sinners are born again and become children of God.[439] Not only does the Holy Spirit do the birthing change of sinners to saints, but he also nurtures them by living within believers.[440] Thus, the Holy Spirit is the most intimate and personal being of the Trinity in that he dwells within believers and is their Counselor.[441] Among humans, this nurturing behavior is something that is most strongly associated with mothers. Believers can grieve the Holy Spirit by rejecting his counsel and being disobedient which seems similar to what mothers experience with wayward children.[442]

In Christian households, husbands are thought of as the head but wives are the heart for they are typically at the center of relationships between husband and children. This is why in many families, the ultimate insults are those directed towards the wife. I believe this is the basis for the statement made by Jesus that insults against him could be forgiven but blasphemy against the Holy Spirit would never be forgiven.[443] Finally, the creation story itself can teach us about how feminine traits are embedded within masculine. Eve was taken out of Adam and it is God's plan for woman to complement and

---

439   He saved us through the washing of rebirth and renewal by the Holy Spirit. (Ti 3:5)

440   Don't you know that you yourselves are God's temple and that God's Spirit lives within you? (1Co 3:16)

441   "And I will ask the Father, and he will give you another Counselor to be with you forever—the Spirit of truth." (Jn 14:16)

442   And do not grieve the Holy Spirit of God with whom you were sealed for the day of redemption. (Eph 4:30)

443   "And so I tell you, every sin and blasphemy will be forgiven men, but the blasphemy against the Holy Spirit will not be forgiven." (Mt 12:31-32)

complete man in marriage.[444] Similarly, the Holy Spirit proceeds from the Father and Son saving sinners and builds up the family of God. It is my prayer that this will help you to better understand that God is more than a Father figure or Jesus incarnate. It is from the awesome complexity of God that he created humans, male and female, to reflect a small part of his infinite being.

---

444 Then the Lord God made a woman from the rib he had taken out of the man, and he brought her to the man. The man said, "This now bone of my bones and flesh of my flesh, she shall be called woman, for she was taken out of man." (Ge 2:22-23)

Discussion Questions

1. Think about God. What image comes to mind? Discuss the reasons why you think this way.

2. When we pray to God, we typically do not pray to the Holy Spirit. Why is this?

3. Most people pray to God using for themselves first; then relatives and friends; then others such as missionaries, nation, poor; then thanks and praise. Why is this?

4. Discuss the following order of prayer:
    a. P=Praise God
    b. R=Repent and Confess Sins
    c. A=Ask for others
    d. Y=Your prayer needs

5. Romans 8:27 says that the Holy Spirit prays for us according to God's will. What does this mean and how does this impact our need to remember to pray for everything we should?

The Gift of Joy

As Easter approaches, I find myself thinking about the death and resurrection of Jesus. The purpose of his life was to offer himself as a sacrifice for the sins of mankind. The Bible says that Jesus became sin for us so that we could be forgiven and found righteous in God's sight.[445] Jesus was so certain of his purpose that he predicted when and how he would die.[446] As believers and followers of Jesus, what is our purpose?

Some would answer that it is to love God while others might say that it is to serve him. The Westminster Shorter Catechism states that man's chief purpose is to glorify God and enjoy him forever. While considering these ideas, Hebrews 12:2 came to mind: "Let us fix our eyes on Jesus, the author and perfecter of our faith, **who for the joy set before him,** endured the cross, scorning its shame, and sat down at the right hand of the throne of God."

Jesus looked beyond the suffering, shame and death he knew was to come and focused on the joy that would result. What is this joy

---

445   God made him who had no sin to be sin for us, so that in him we might become the righteousness of God. (2Co 5:21)

446   As you know, the Passover is two days away—and the Son of Man will be handed over to be crucified." (Mt 26:2)

that so motivated him? The Bible says that there is great joy in heaven whenever a sinner repents.[447] Likewise, the Lord rewards good works and there is joy in hearing him say "Well done good and faithful servant." Therefore, Jesus anticipated the joy that would happen when each person repents and is saved. He also looked forward to the joy that would result from each good work done by believers in obedience and motivated by love.

The Bible says that we love God because he first loved us.[448] Ephesians 2:1-10 tells us that by nature we are rebellious towards God and are born spiritually dead. It is by his love and grace that he brings us to faith and reconciliation. God has even planned our good works![449] What then is our purpose?

We can give him joy! What a wonderful God we have who honors sinners like us by giving us the ability to give him pleasure! He rejoices and experiences joy as we respond to him in repentance, love and good works that bring him glory! Give Jesus the gift of joy for he is looking forward to it.

---

447 In the same way, I tell you, there is rejoicing in the presence of the angels of God over one sinner who repents. (Lk 15:10)

448 We love because he first loved us. (1Jn 4:19)

449 For we are God's workmanship, created in Christ Jesus to do good works, which God prepared in advance for us to do. (Eph 2:10)

Discussion Questions

1. What is the difference between joy and happiness?

2. Why are faith, obedience, and love dependent on the presence and work of the Holy Spirit? Is the joy of God different?

3. What is the role of man's will in faith, salvation, and love? How about spiritual knowledge, obedience, and joy?

4. Discuss how seeking to give God joy is better than making obedience or even love the ultimate goal of our relationship with God and the purpose of our lives.

5. How do you know deep inside yourself that you have pleased God after exercising your spiritual gifts?

6. Read Nehemiah 8:10. How does the joy of the Lord give strength?

7. Psalm 116:5 says "Precious in the sight of the Lord is the death of his saints." Discuss what this means related to giving God the gift of joy.

The Passion of Christ

What is the passion of Christ? Many would say it is the period of intense suffering in the life of Jesus from the Garden of Gethsemane to the crucifixion. To others the passion of Christ evokes images of gruesome punishment depicted in movies such as Mel Gibson's *The Passion of The Christ*. Certainly these views are correct, but I have discovered that there is much more to the passion of Christ.

What does it mean to be passionate? Webster's Dictionary defines passion as "extreme, compelling emotion or intense emotional drive."

What was the source of the passion of Christ? It was his intense love for mankind. The great love of Jesus resulted in his extreme commitment to walk a very precise and narrow path to redeem mankind.

For the sake of restoring humans to fellowship with God, he made himself nothing, taking the very nature of a servant by being made in human likeness.[450] His passionate love caused him to leave the glory of heaven to take human form and live an obedient life of self-sacrifice required by the holiness of God. Only such a selfless life could produce the pure and innocent blood sacrifice required to cover the sins of those who put their faith in him.[451]

The passion of Christ was directed by the Father's will and resulted in a life whose purpose was death on the cross.[452] Jesus was dedicated to accomplish the requirements foretold by prophecies and the will of the Father. In Matthew 4:8-9, the devil offered Jesus the kingdoms of the world in exchange for his worship. This offer represented a way for Jesus to establish his kingdom on earth without the cross. It may have seemed like an easy short cut, but Jesus was passionate to accomplish the exact plan of the Father and so rejected the devil's offer.

In John 6:14-15, a crowd tried to make Jesus a king by force, but he again rejected their attempt because it would have deviated from the cross. The final words of Jesus from the cross were a triumphant proclamation. Like a runner crossing the finish line in agony, yet with great emotion in overcoming obstacles, Jesus says "It is finished!"[453]

The passion of Christ originated in love, was directed by the purpose of God and was lived in dependence on the presence of

---

450 Who being in very nature God, did not consider equality with God something to be grasped, but made himself nothing, taking the very nature of a servant, being made in human likeness. And being found in appearance as a man, he humbled himself and became obedient to death—even death on a cross! (Php 2:6-7)

451 For God so loved the world that he gave his one and only Son, that whoever believes in him shall not perish but have everlasting life. (Jn 3:16) In him we have redemption through his blood, the forgiveness of sins, in accordance with the riches of God's grace that he lavished on us with all wisdom and understanding. (Eph 1:7)

452 Now my heart is troubled, and what shall I say? Father, save me from this hour? No, it was for this very reason I came to this hour. (Jn 12:27)

453 When he had received the drink, Jesus said, "It is finished." (Jn 19:30)

God. Jesus declared that every word that he said was given to him by the Father who commanded him what to say and how to say it.[454] In order for this to happen, Jesus lived every moment in the presence of the Father. Every thought, word and action of Jesus was given to him by the Father.[455]

The passion of Christ was energized by the power of God. Jesus healed the sick, restored the paralyzed, calmed the sea, fed the multitudes and raised the dead through the power of God. Even when he was handed over to the mob led by Judas, he spoke and they fell backwards onto the ground.[456] Jesus was always in control of his life. He said that more than twelve legions, or in excess of thirty-six thousand angels, would respond to his commands.[457]

Jesus was not just a good man who fell victim to evil circumstances. On the contrary, he predicted the manner of his death and the time and place chosen by the Father.[458] Jesus was not a powerless victim. He embraced death to accomplish our redemption and rose from the dead in power and majesty!

The life of Christ has set a pattern for living a passionate life for him. Believers in Jesus experience a spiritual birth that results in the

---

454 For I did not speak of my own accord, but the Father who sent me commanded me what to say and how to say it. (Jn 12:49)

455 Whoever has my commands and obeys them, he is the one who loves me. He who loves me will be loved by my Father, and I too will love him and show myself to him. (Jn 14:21)

456 When Jesus said, "I am he," they drew back and fell to the ground. (Jn 18:6)

457 Do you think I cannot call on my Father, and he will at once put at my disposal more than six legions of angels? (Mt 26:53).

458 As you know, the Passover is two days away—and the Son of Man will be handed over to be crucified. (Mt 26:2)

indwelling presence of the Holy Spirit.[459] Therefore, believers have everything needed to live a passionate life for Christ. Why then are there so few passionate Christians? I believe the answer lies in the fact that few Christians follow the pattern of Christ's life.

First and foundational to everything else is the importance of building a love relationship with Jesus. Deuteronomy 6:5 says, "Love the Lord your God with all your heart and with all your soul and with all your strength."

This is a lofty command but one that is critical for believers to strive to attain.

The love of Jesus is the most precious, personal and intense of relationships. Believers must learn to live in daily, if not moment by moment, dependence on Jesus, seeking his will and experiencing his presence. This begins with setting thoughts on God. Proverbs 23:7 says that we are defined by what we think about.

Paul says that believers are to set their minds on what is pure, lovely, excellent, and praiseworthy and God will be with them.[460] It may not be possible to do this all the time, but the key is to find the places, ways, and times where God is presently experienced and build on these. The more God is experienced, the more your mind will dwell on him and with him. This produces ever increasing praise, worship, and thoughts of God that translate into actions that express love and seek to honor him.

---

459 Do you not know that your body is a temple of the Holy Spirit, who is in you, whom you have received from God? You are not your own; you were bought at a price. Therefore, honor God with your body. (1Cor 6:19)
Do you not know that your body is a temple of the Holy Spirit, who is in you, whom you have received from God? You are not your own; you were bought at a price. Therefore, honor God with your body. (1Cor 6:19)

460 Finally brothers, whatever is true, whatever is noble, whatever is right, whatever is pure, whatever is lovely, whatever is admirable—if anything is excellent or praiseworthy—think about such things. Whatever you have learned or received or heard from me, or seen in me—put it into practice. And the God of peace will be with you. (Php 4:8-9)

In practicing being in the presence of God, the purpose of God is discovered. This is summed up in the great commission where Jesus commands his disciples to go and tell others everything that he has revealed to them.[461] This is a key to understanding and following God's plan for our lives. The knowledge and experiences that God gives us will help us discover his purpose for our lives. Sharing personal encounters with God makes for passionate expressions of teaching, praise, and worship!

Finally, the power of God is manifest in actions stemming from the love, purpose, and presence of God. God energizes us resulting in heightened joy and boldness to do his will. Evidence of the power of God revealed through believers includes unexpected insights and blessings. An example that I have experienced in teaching is through feedback I have received. I have been told of some idea or insight attributed to my teaching that I did not intend. In such cases, I have been blessed by the fact that God took my ideas and expanded them beyond what I intended.

Other evidence of the power of God flowing through believers includes changed lives and spiritual growth based on increased faith, wisdom, and knowledge. Ever present with the power of God is his love that transforms our lives, inspiring us to be passionate in our pursuit of Christ!

---

461 Therefore go and make disciples of all nations, baptizing them in the name of the Father and of the Son and of the Holy Spirit, and teaching them to obey everything I have commanded you. And surely I am with you always, to the very end of the age. (Mt 28:19-20)

Discussion Questions

1. Sports fans seem to have more passion than many Christians. Why is this?

2. The word fan derives from fanatic. What are some of the fanatic practices of sports fans? Draw some parallel behaviors that might help us understand what fanatic Christians might look and act like. For example, sports fans look forward to the next game. Christians with passion should look forward to Sunday worship. What do they like to talk about? How do they dress and act? Do they have unity of purpose?

3. Make a list of emotions that are typical in being passionate about something. What causes these emotions? Is it possible to be passionate about something without being emotional?

4. Sports fans that are most passionate usually spend time studying statistics, thinking about past and future games as well as news about players. By doing these things they become experts. How is this like the passion of Christians? Does this explain why there are fewer passionate Christians than sports fans?

5. What are some ways that you can become a more passionate Christian?

Trinity or Triune God

The concept of God being three persons in one is referred to as the Trinity and is an essential part of the Christian faith. Although the word "Trinity" is not found in the Bible, there are many places in scripture that support this concept. The plurality or multi-person nature of God is illustrated in Genesis 1:26 where God says, "Let **us** make man in **our** image, in **our** likeness." When Adam and Eve sinned, God said that man had become "like **us**", having knowledge of good and evil.[462] When God sends Isaiah to speak to the Israelites, God asks him "Who shall **I** send? And who will go for **us**?" This shifting of the use of **I** and **us** does not make sense unless God is one being and more than one person.[463] The persons of God the Father and Son are mentioned as creators of the earth in Proverbs 30:4.

When Jesus ascends into heaven, he gives his disciples a commission to go and make disciples of all nations, baptizing them

---

462 And the Lord God said, "The man has now become like one of us, knowing good and evil. He must not be allowed to reach out his hand and take also from the tree of life and eat, and live forever." (Ge 3:22)

463 Then I heard the voice of the Lord saying, "Whom shall I send? And who will go for us?" And I said, "Here am I. Send me!" (Isa 6:8)

in the name of the Father and of the Son and of the Holy Spirit.[464] By this statement, Jesus testifies to the triune nature of God. In John 15:26, Jesus further tells his disciples that he will send the Counselor from the Father. This Counselor is the Holy Spirit who testifies about Jesus. In this one verse, Jesus refers to the three persons of God.

The idea that God can exist in many believers through the presence of the Holy Spirit testifies to the fact that the Holy Spirit and God are one person.[465] This verse also says that God exists simultaneously in believers through the presence of the Holy Spirit so that not only is God multi-persons, but these persons can be in many people or places simultaneously.

During the baptism of Jesus, the Spirit of God descends from heaven and the voice of God the Father speaks from heaven saying, "This is my Son, whom I love; with him I am well pleased".[466] These three persons of God are the three who testify and are in agreement in 1 John 5:7-8.

Man is a triune being composed of body, soul, and mind.[467] Since man is made in God's image and likeness, man reflects that triune nature of God in his three part nature. While this reflection is not directly comparable to God since man is three component parts versus three distinct persons, I believe God teaches man through his creation that man has separate yet co-existing parts just as God is three separate but co-existing persons.

---

464   Therefore go and make disciples of all nations, baptizing them in the name of the Father and of the Son and of the Holy Spirit, (Mt 28:19)

465   And in him you too are being built together to become a dwelling in which God lives by his Spirit. (Eph 2:22)

466   As soon as Jesus was baptized, he went up out of the water. At that moment heaven was opened, and he saw the Spirit of God descending like a dove and lighting on him. And a voice from heaven said, "This is my Son, whom I love; with him I am well pleased." (Mt 3:16-17)

467   May God himself, the God of peace, sanctify you through and through. May your whole spirit, soul and body be kept blameless at the coming of our Lord Jesus Christ. (1Th 5:23)

Jesus taught his disciples that he and the Father were one in the sense of being the same entity. This is illustrated in John 12:44-45, where Jesus says that belief in him is equivalent to belief in the Father and seeing him is the same as seeing the Father. Jesus said when you look at him you are looking at God the Father.[468] The fullness of God in bodily form is found in Jesus Christ.[469]

"May the Lord direct your hearts into God's love and Christ's perseverance".[470] This verse draws distinctions between "Lord," "God," and "Christ" that do not make sense unless God is three distinct persons. Jesus Christ is God and his Son.[471] The Holy Spirit is distinct from God the Father and God the Son and is referred to as a person (the Counselor) rather than a force or thing.[472]

More evidence of the triune nature of God is seen in the threefold repetition of the word "Holy" by worshipping angels at the throne of God.[473] The three persons of God are mentioned in 2 Corinthians 13:14, where Paul closes this epistle with a threefold blessing to believers, mentioning the grace of Jesus Christ, the love of God, and the fellowship of the Holy Spirit.

---

468   Philip said, "Lord, show us the Father and that will be enough for us." Jesus answered, "Don't you know me, Philip, even after I have been among you such a long time? Anyone who has seen me has seen the Father. How can you say, "Show us the Father?" (Jn 14:8-9)

469   For in Christ all the fullness of the Deity lives in bodily form, (Col 2:9)

470   May the Lord direct your hearts into God's love and Christ's perseverance. (2Th 3:5)

471   We also know that the Son of God has come and has given us understanding, so that we may know him who is true. And we are in him who is true - even in his Son Jesus Christ. He is the true God and eternal life. (1Jn 5:20)

472   When the Counselor comes, whom I will send to you from the Father, the Spirit of truth who goes out from the Father, he will testify about me. (Jn 15:26)

473   And they were calling to one another: "Holy, holy, holy is the Lord Almighty; the whole earth is full of his glory." (Isa 6:3)

Discussion Questions

1. What are some denominations that claim to be Christian but deny the Trinity?

2. What are some common objections that are raised regarding the Trinity? How do you answer these objections?

3. What are the similarities and differences between man's body, mind and spirit and the Trinity?

4. Do you think God created man in his image to teach us something about himself? If so, what?

5. Why do people seem to have more of a problem with the Trinity than with the omnipresence of God?

6. The Triune nature of God is foreign to humans and so hard to understand. There are aspects of God that are like humans such as that man is made in the image of God. Also, Jesus is God in human flesh. Man relates to God through his human likeness since this is what we can understand. What are some of the dangers of defining or confining God to human qualities that we can understand?

When Prayers Seem To Fail

Have you ever felt like you are talking to yourself when you pray or that your prayers don't seem to go any further than your ceiling? What causes this? There are several reasons for this. First is the belief that the quality of our prayers depend on how we feel about them. When we are hopeful and optimistic, we tend to think better of ourselves and that God is listening. When we are depressed or worried, we are more likely to become frustrated, give up or wonder where God is. However, the Bible says that we are to pray without ceasing which means that God expects us to pray whether we feel like it or not.[474] God is ever present and unchanging so he is not influenced by how we feel.

God may not answer our prayers because they are not in accord with his will and plans. Isaiah 55:8-9 say that God's thoughts are not like those of mankind nor are his ways like those of man but rather just as the heavens are higher than the earth so are God's

---

474   pray continually. (1Th 5:17)

thoughts, view and ways beyond ours. Therefore, God may choose not to answer our prayers or he may answer them in ways that are different than what we prayed.

God may not answer our prayers because we are holding onto sinful ways. Psalm 66:18-19 says that when we cherish or hold onto sin that God will not listen to our prayers. When we choose to hold onto sin, we rebel against God and evil rules in this part of our lives. Therefore, we must confess our sins and forsake them if we expect God to listen to our prayers.[475]

Sometimes God says yes but the answer is delayed or slow in coming. One possible reason for this is that God wants teach us to trust in him and learn dependence upon him so that he can direct our paths.[476] Finally, we need to remember that spiritual warfare is raging throughout this world. Satan and his demons are inciting rebellion and exerting their will. They do this through evil temptations of this world such as the pride of life which is excessive focus on getting more and better things or money. Also, evil can ensnare us through the pursuit of power and influence at the expense of relationships as well as through the weaknesses of our human nature such as selfishness, lust, greed and envy.

---

475   If my people, who are called by my name, will humble themselves and
        pray and seek my face and turn from their wicked ways, then will I hear
        from heaven and will forgive their sin and will heal their land. (2Ch 7:14)
        If we confess our sins, he is faithful and just and will forgive us our sins
        and purify us from all unrighteousness. (1Jn 1:9)

476   Trust in the Lord with all your heart and lean not on your own
        understanding; in all your ways acknowledge him and he will you're your
        paths straight. (Pr 3:5-6)

Daniel fasted and prayed for twenty-four days before he received an answer to his prayers.[477] An angel appeared to him on the twenty-fourth day and told Daniel that, from the first day that he prayed, the angel was sent from God with the answers. However, the angel was held up by a demon called the prince of the Persian kingdom. This angel could not get through until help arrived in the form of the angel Michael presumably because Daniel continued to persist in prayer. This is challenging and encouraging because it shows the importance of persisting in prayer until answers are realized. How many times have we stopped praying because we have not seen any results? I wonder how many angels are stuck battling opposing demons because we do not persist in prayer.

---

477   Then he continued, "Do not be afraid, Daniel. Since the first day that you set your mind to gain understanding and to humble yourself before your God, your words were heard, and I have come in response to them. But the prince of the Persian kingdom resisted me twenty-one days. Then Michael, one of the chief princes, came to help me, because I was detained there with the king of Persia. (Da 10:12-14)

Discussion Questions

1. Many times we launch into prayers with very little thought or quiet time. Why is this?

2. Discuss the difference between head praying and heart praying. Which do we tend to do most often?

3. What is the purpose before praying at certain times of the day such as when you wake up, eat, sleep and read the Bible?

4. What role does fasting play in praying?

5. Do you keep a prayer list? Do you keep a praise list that tracks when and how your prayers have been answered?

6. I have found that it is many times more difficult to pray with a spouse or family members than with others. Why is this?

7. What are the various reasons for praying? What type of prayers do you do most often? Why?

8. When do pray aloud in your daily routine? Do you pray aloud in public places? Why or why not?

9. What attitudes should we come to God in prayer?

10. What are some reasons we become discouraged so that we do not pray as often or fervently as we should?

Why Go to Church?

Every Sunday many people go to church, while others are sleeping or engaged in other weekend activities. Since our weekends are limited, should we spend part of them in church? First, let's look at some of the popular reasons for not going:

Church is boring.

It is repetitive, predictable, and a meaningless ritual. I would rather sleep in. I work hard all week and I deserve it! Sure, church is repetitive, but so is life. The days of our lives are structured around cycles of work, eating, family, and recreation times. Any of these activities can become boring if we don't strive to find something interesting or enjoyable about them. Sunday mornings at church are times to make new friends and renew old ones; to learn about the Bible and share problems, as well as to thank God for another week of life. The objective in going to church is to seek to build our relationship with God and others. Some people go to church to fulfill an obligation through some ritual. Such activities are reduced to actions without meaning. Church worship is all about an encounter with God and others; it changes who we are. Not going to church on a Sunday morning because you deserve a sleep-in does not explain why you miss church on Saturday or Sunday night. The problem is much deeper than the time of the day—it is a matter of selfishness.

Why bother to go to church when all they want is money?

If you choose to get involved in any kind of group, be it the PTA, Boy Scouts or whatever, it will cost you in time and money. It is true that, if you don't get involved in anything, you will have maximum control of your time and money. However, you will miss friendships and opportunities to be a good influence in the lives of others. Each of us must decide where to spend our time and money. Each of us will either invest it in some purpose or waste it on the pleasures of the moment. Jesus said that there is an eternal investment that will not fade, rust, or decay when we do good works that show our love for God and others.[478] Ponder this! You do not control your life. You cannot guarantee that you will be alive the next week, day, hour or moment. Human life is a gift from God and he controls the measure of it.[479] Our intelligence, talents, and appearance are largely determined by genetics (which is to say by God, who made us individually unique). Therefore, who we are, when and where we are born and how long we live are gifts from God. Is it unreasonable for God to ask for a portion of it to acknowledge him and his sovereignty?

---

478   Do not store up for yourselves treasures on earth, where moth and rust destroy, and where thieves break in and steal. But store up for yourselves treasures in heaven, where moth and rust do not destroy, and where thieves do not break in and steal. (Mt 6:19-20)

479   your eyes saw my unformed body. All the days ordained for me were written in your book before one of them came to be. (Ps 139:16)

People who go to church are a bunch of hypocrites!

Church goers pretend to be good for a few hours on Sunday morning but they are like everyone else the rest of the week. A common misunderstanding about church is that it should somehow make us better people. As discussed above, it is not the action of going to church but the encounters with God and others that change our lives for the better. Most people who go to church do not understand this and thus do not seek to have life changing experiences through worship and church activities.

Christians are humans who believe that Jesus is God and that he has made us acceptable to himself by paying the penalty for our sins on the cross.[480] Therefore, what makes Christians unique is not the outward appearance but what God has done on the inside by changing the soul and mind.[481] Those who sincerely call upon Jesus to save them from their sins experience a spiritual birth that gradually transforms the mind and behavior conforming us to his will.[482]

Christians can be seen to be hypocrites more easily than someone who does not profess any beliefs because Christian standards are

---

480   For the wages of sin is death, but the gift of God is eternal life in Jesus Christ our Lord. (Ro 6:23)

481   Therefore, if anyone is in Christ, he is a new creation; the old has gone, the new has come! (2Co 5:17)

482   Yet to all who received him, to those who believed in his name, he gave the right to become the children of God—children born not of natural descent, nor of human decision or a husband's will, but born of God. (Jn 1:12-13)
Therefore, I urge you, brothers, in view of God's mercy, to offer your bodies as living sacrifices, holy and pleasing to God—this is your spiritual act of worship. Do not conform any longer to the pattern of this world, but be transformed by the renewing of your mind. Then you will be able to test and approve what God's will is—his good, pleasing and perfect will. (Ro 12:1-2)

defined in the Bible whereas personal standards can be changed to fit circumstances or are unknown to others. The bottom line is that all humans are hypocrites because we all fail to consistently live up to any standards of behavior that are defined. The difference is that Jesus forgives the hypocrisy of believers and has sent his Holy Spirit to guide and transform those who know him as Savior and confess him as Lord.[483]

Church is unnecessary since private prayer and Bible study can be done without others.

The Bible says that believers must not keep apart from other believers.[484] It is true that we are influenced by, and become like, the people with whom we associate. Also, by getting together, common beliefs are affirmed and ways to overcome problems are shared. There are three spiritual pillars to having a strong Christian life: personal prayer, Bible study, and fellow believers. To rely on less than all three is like trying to sit on a one- or two-legged stool. Three legs are needed for a firm foundation and proper function.

Churches impose a bunch of rules and then make you feel guilty if you don't measure up.

One of the biggest reasons for the breakdown of families is the lack of moral standards. Most people who call themselves Christians

---

483 That if you confess with your mouth, "Jesus is Lord," and believe in your heart that God raised him from the dead, you will be saved. For it is with your heart that you believe and are justified, and it is with your mouth that you confess and are saved. (Ro 10:9-10)

484 And let us consider how we may spur one another on toward love and good deeds. Let us not give up meeting together, as some are in the habit of doing, but let us encourage one another—and all the more as you see the Day approaching. (Heb 10:24-25)

cannot even list the Ten Commandments much less live by them. Without moral standards, it is easier to do your own thing and not feel guilty about it. Guilt is part of our conscience and is a gift from God to help us do what is right. It is true that sometimes people make us feel guilty. During these times it is important to seek God's view through prayer and reading the Bible. This means it is necessary to be familiar enough with the Bible to discern whether it is God or others making us feel guilty. I am convinced that there are many Christians who are doing good works out of guilt rather than because they are motivated to express their love for God.

Discussion Questions

1. Do you look forward to going to church each week? List the reasons why or why not.

2. What does worship mean to you? How do you know that you have worshipped God when you leave church?

3. What are some essential elements that you consider necessary for worship? Discuss the reasons why.

4. Do you prepare for worship? If not, explain why. If so, how do you do this? Do you think there is a relationship between meaningful worship and how we prepare?

5. Is it necessary for Christians to be involved in the ministries of the local church?

6. How does one decide what church ministries are a good fit with which to become involved?

7. Do you think that church services should sometimes include messages about giving money and stewardship?

8. Do you agree or disagree with the following: Christian churches in America are run like businesses.

9. The following is a blog post on a web page related to church attendance: "Religion is not important. Good will, common sense, and logical thinking are all we need, not illogical cults like religion.

Long live science." Do you think this type of thinking is widespread and affects church attendance?

10. What are the reasons why those who claim to be associated with a Christian denomination do not go to church every week? What are some solutions to these reasons?

Why Not Look at Pornography?

I have seen my share of centerfolds in times past but I no longer think that viewing such materials is healthy or worthwhile. In today's society, there is a popular view that "as long as it doesn't hurt anyone, it's OK" or "If it feels good—DO IT!" I have weighed the pros and cons of looking at so-called "soft" pornography and have reached several conclusions.

First, humans (especially males) are sexually aroused through visual stimuli, hence the strong appeal of this type of magazine. This form of stimulation is doomed to frustration because the viewer cannot have the woman or object that the photos portray. It is like a hungry person looking at pictures of food. I would rather eat a hamburger that is at home than to look at pictures of gourmet food that I cannot eat. This is a subtle form of mental torture and ends in frustration.

Second, unhealthy comparisons are made between one's mate and the pornography. Why isn't my wife bigger here and smaller there, have different facial features, or look like that in a swimsuit or nightgown? The Bible says that man is to rejoice in the wife of his youth, to be enthralled by her appearance and ravished by her love.[485] Looking at carefully selected and unattainable beauties tends to make one dissatisfied with one's mate and encourages sexual fantasies that can ultimately devastate marital sexual satisfaction.

Third, these women are dehumanized objects of lust rather than people. They are idealized by placing them in provocative poses and by hiding or touching up imperfections. They are impersonal and unattainable and therefore an illusion. I ask myself: whose wife, sister, or mother are these women? I would view them differently if they were someone I knew or loved as a friend, relative, or spouse.

Finally, some may say that looking does no harm, but God says that it is sinful for a man to look upon a woman (other than one's spouse) with lust regardless of whether there is ever any physical relationship.[486] This makes virtually all men sinners, which is precisely what the Bible says.[487] Some may say that they can look at attractive, naked women without lust and admire the beauty of the human body. The Bible also says that it is sinful to look upon the nakedness of another man's wife, mother, or sister.[488] Also, one of the Ten Commandments says, "You shall not covet your neighbor's wife".[489]

---

485 May your fountain be blessed, and may you rejoice in the wife of your youth. A loving doe, a graceful deer—may her breasts satisfy you always, may you ever be captivated by her love. (Pr 5:18-19)

486 But I tell you that anyone who looks at a woman lustfully has already committed adultery with her in his heart. (Mt 5:28)

487 for all have sinned and fall short of the glory of God, (Ro 3:23)

488 No one is to approach any close relative to have sexual relations, I am the Lord. (Lev 18:6)

489 You shall not covet your neighbor's wife. You shall not set your desire on your neighbor's house or land, his manservant or maidservant, his ox or donkey, or anything else that belongs to your neighbor. (Dt 5:21)

The one who made us knows us best. He has told us, in not so many words, that looking at pornography fills our minds with images that make us restless and frustrated. It also offends our Maker.

Discussion Questions

1. Most Christians would not allow pornography magazines into their homes. However, similar visual images do routinely intrude into our homes through TV, movies and magazine advertisements. Where do you draw the line on what is acceptable or not? Do you have the same standards for yourself as for your children? If not, why not?

2. How do you deal with foul or sexually explicit language used in some TV shows and movies?

3. Do you think sexual images and language are affecting our society? If so, discuss the changes they may have caused.

4. What do you think about art that involves nude images of men and women?

5. Do you think that pornographic pictures de-humanize the person portrayed? Does it have a de-humanizing effect on the viewer?

6. Do you think that hetero-sexual pornography leads to a desire to watch other forms of sexual activity such as groups of adults or child pornography?

Bibliography

About Alcohol Facts, The National Center on Addiction and Substance Abuse (CASA) at Columbia University in 2005, http://www.about-alcohol-facts.com/

About.com Marriage, Cohabitation Facts & Statistics, http://marriage.about.com/od/cohabitation/qt/cohabfacts.htm

Alcoholism: Clinical & Experimental Research, 6-14-04; Berman, Jessica. Moderate alcohol consumption benefits heart, U.S. government says. Voice of America News, 6-16-04, http://www2.potsdam.edu/hansondj/InTheNews/MedicalReports/Longevity/1088617919.html

All About The Journey, Evolution & The Fossil Record, Luther D. Sutherland, *Darwin's Enigma: Fossils and Other Problems*, 4th edition, Master Books, 1988, 9 http://www.allaboutthejourney.org/evolution-and-the-fossil-record.htm

Answers, World History, Middle English *helle,* from Old English, http://www.answers.com/topic/hell

Clarifying Christianity, What is Baptism? http://www. clarifyingchristianity.com/get_wet.shtml

Neatorama, Bizzare Fortune Telling Methods, Alex Santoso, Tuesday, August 21, 2007, http://www.neatorama. com/2007/08/21/bizarre-fortune-telling-methods/

PBS NineNet, Frontline, Gambling Facts & Stats, http://www.pbs. org/wgbh/pages/frontline/shows/gamble/etc/facts.html

Ross, Hugh Norman. *Beyond The Cosmos: The Extra-dimensionality of God: What Recent Discoveries in Astronomy and Physics Reveal About the Glory and Love of God.* Colorado Springs: NAVPRESS, 1996

Scofield, C. I. ed. *The New Scofield Study Bible: New International Version.* Copyright 1984 by the International Bible Society. Used by permission of the Oxford University Press. All rights reserved.

The Forgiveness Web, Forgiveness Quotations, http://www. forgivenessweb.com/RdgRm/Quotationpage.html

The Vanishing Tatoo, Facts & Statistics, Harris Poll #15, February12,2008, http://www.vanishingtattoo.com/tattoo_ facts.htm#Harris_Poll

Author's Note

My greatest credential is my daily and systematic study of the Bible over the past thirty plus years. My motivation for doing this comes from a deep love and commitment I have to experience ever more of the transforming presence of God in my life. The foundation for this motivation is a spiritual birth that has fundamentally changed me. Prior to this birth, there was only "I", but since there is always "we". Over the years, my knowledge and experience of God have increased as a result of regular Bible study, prayer, and interaction with other believers. I have been a deacon, taught Sunday School classes and small groups, spoken in churches and conventions as a Gideon, and have performed many good deeds that I would never have considered by myself. I have learned that these credentials or accomplishments are worthless unless they originate from and are an expression of the love I have for God. Indeed, these very same actions can become a hindrance in that the status, accomplishments, and praise of others can become the motivation rather than an expression of love.

In America, copies of the Bible are plentiful, but it remains a book that relatively few have read. Therefore, most people do not know what it says. We have put our trust in theologians or religious leaders, which has resulted in the popular belief that the Bible is hard to understand due to many interpretations, or that it contains contradictions or myths. It is not necessary to have a theological degree or training to understand the Bible. The essentials are a born again faith in Jesus Christ and disciplined study. Seek the advice and counsel of theologians, Christian books, and other believers, but do not be bound by them. Let the Bible always rule in seeking God's message and perspective. My hope is that this book will demonstrate that the Bible presents truths on a wide variety of practical and theological issues that come from the mind of God.